I Survived and Thrived

The Great Depression, Discrimination, WWII

Joseph Sorge

authorHOUSE®

AuthorHouse™
1663 Liberty Drive
Bloomington, IN 47403
www.authorhouse.com
Phone: 1-800-839-8640

First published by AuthorHouse 9/11/2009

ISBN: 978-1-4490-0714-0 (e)
ISBN: 978-1-4490-0712-6 (sc)
ISBN: 978-1-4490-0713-3 (hc)

To order book call Authorhouse 1-888-280-7715

Printed in the United States of America
Bloomington, Indiana

This book is printed on acid-free paper.

To Margaret, my loving wife of fifty-six years. I thank her for her assistance and encouragement in writing this book. Without her in my life, I would not have become the person I am.

Special thanks to my sons, Joe and Tony, and their families for all the love and joy they have brought to me.

CONTENTS

INTRODUCTION

This book is a look back on life from my perspective as an eighty-four-year-old veteran of World War II. I begin my adventures at age ten in Newark, New Jersey, and take you through my travels of the world, including a tour of duty on the USS *Missouri*, where I witnessed the signing of Japan's surrender by Foreign Minister Mamoru Shigemitsu.

I have seen a lot in my lifetime and want to share my experiences and life's lessons, particularly with those of you who may not understand what life was like during the Great Depression.

CHAPTER 1

MY CHILDHOOD DURING THE DEPRESSION

I will never forget the time I witnessed a murder—it was in a neighborhood noted for its violence. My uncle and I were in a pastry shop when we heard gunfire outside. We ran out to see what was happening, and we found a man lying in the street, bleeding from his head and with blood spattered all over him. Another man was on his knees, holding his arm; a bullet had hit him. My uncle and I were both shocked to witness this incident. Two women were screaming—we learned that they were the wives of these men. Within minutes, many spectators were at the scene, and the police arrived shortly afterward. My uncle and I were too stunned to move. I was only ten years old when this happened, but I never forgot it; the incident is ingrained in my brain.

My uncle later told me the reason for the shooting. The two men involved had been competing for dominance of their personal transactions, trying to gain favor from the underworld. I was too young to know what that was all about. This happened around 1935, in the middle of the Great Depression. Money was very scarce, and many people were desperate. I guess some people would take very dangerous chances in order to survive. A life of poverty and lack of an education would breathe violence into many young men. I was lucky to have parents and grandparents who kept us above the poverty line. Some of the children that I grew up with were not so fortunate; still, their parents kept them in line, and they grew up all right. All I know is that most of us had fear ingrained in our brains, and we grew up on the right side of the law. We had to show respect to our elders.

I was born in Glen Ridge, New Jersey, in 1925, a few years before the beginning of the Great Depression. My grandparents were immigrants from Italy who arrived in this country in the late 1800s. I give them credit for coming to this country without knowing what to expect. Unlike many immigrants, however, my family was fortunate in that they had some education, which gave them a small advantage. My grandfather graduated from high school, his sister was a schoolteacher in the old country, and his brother could speak English fluently. My mother and father were born in America, and both spoke English and Italian. My father did not have much of an education because he was the eldest in his family and had to go to work at a young age to help support the family. The Depression made it hard on many families. Welfare did not exist during that era. They had "city assistance," but anyone receiving the subsidy was ashamed to admit it. My family, however, was able to survive because my grandfather and father were in the wholesale importing produce business, and they were able to keep it running during the hard times.

I remember when I was at the New York World's Fair in 1939, and my family was talking about a couple of our relatives who had been waiting five years to get into the United States. Now, immigrants can enter the United States within minutes, and the government provides special classes for learning of English. Back in my day, we had to teach immigrants ourselves. That was seventy years ago, though. Conditions change.

My parents could speak both English and Italian, but they only spoke English to my brothers and me—although I learned some Italian words from my grandmother. When relatives would visit, they would speak in Italian, too, and I would hear certain words and remember them. Later, I would ask my mother to translate for me. Today I understand a little Italian but not enough to hold a conversation.

During the Depression, life was often very hard. One day, someone knocked on our door. I answered, and there stood an elderly man in raggedy clothes, but he had a distinguished look. My mother came to the door and asked the man what he wanted.

"I'm hungry," the man said. "Can you help?"

Without hesitation, my mom directed him to the kitchen table. She made him breakfast as he told us his tale. He explained that he had worked for a company that had gone bust, and he had been out of work for several months. When he finished eating, my mother gave him a bag of fruit and some bread, and a couple of dollars. Then he was on his way. My mother reminded me then that some people were suffering. Although that happened in 1934, I still remember the incident.

During the Depression, I saw a movie in which a pastor was preaching to his congregation as members of the congregation passed the collection plate. The pastor told the people, "Please let us hear the rustle of bills, instead of the ringing of coins." At that time, things were very bad, and all people could afford to give were coins. Even though it was over seventy-five years ago, I still remember that scene in the movie. The preachers in those days had to hustle the people to give more money, but it was like trying to get blood out of a stone. The public was just plain broke. All people could think about was survival.

When I think back to the Depression, it seems to me that people were friendlier to each other. Today, having money has made people more hostile toward each other because those who have money feel superior. Yet, with all the money, they are not happy. In the old days, my grandfather would give one of my uncles ten dollars to buy meat and pasta. That would be enough food to feed fifteen men. My cousin drove a produce truck that was fitted with wooden benches to accommodate those fifteen men, including my grandfather. I would sit in the cab with my cousin, and we would drive to the farm in Flemington, New Jersey. It was about fifty miles from the city. When we got to the farm, the farmer would supply the men with a clean wooden board to put the pasta on later.

The farmer would also have about twenty chickens to be de-feathered and cleaned by the men. Everyone helped with the chores. My grandfather would pay the farmer for the chickens because he had a little more money than the rest of the men. The cost was probably about thirty-five cents each. They would build a fire and make some kind of a barbecue stove. A couple of men would make the homemade pasta and the gravy. At first, I wondered what the clean board was to be used for, but I found out that they would put the pasta on this very long board and play a comical game. The rules were that the men had to eat the pasta with their hands behind their backs. It was a sight to see—seniors slurping pasta and getting their faces full of red gravy! They had plenty of fun. Then, they would eat the meat and chickens. They would also drink homemade wine. Then, they would play their guitars, and my grandfather would chime in with his mandolin. They had a good time, and the cost was, at most, thirty-five dollars for all of them to eat well, enjoy some entertainment, and stay the night. They slept in the farmer's barn, and my cousin and I slept in the truck. We did outing at least three times every summer. That was two days spent without women, and we all had a wonderful time.

There was closeness then because everyone needed each other, more or less. Not today. Many people think they can have a good time by getting drunk and taking drugs to get a high. In the end, they will be put a low six feet under before their time.

Despite the Depression, I still attended a private Catholic school. The nuns pounded religion into all of the students. They were strict but, all in all, they made sure we learned. If students did not study, then the nuns would harass them harshly. After school, my grandmother would send me out to do errands, which included buying the groceries. In those days, there weren't any large supermarkets. I had to go to the chicken market for freshly killed chickens, to the coffee store for coffee, and to the butcher for meat. Bread and milk were delivered to the house—that saved me a couple of trips. After the chores were finished on Saturday—and depending on whether my mother was in a good mood—I would get twenty-five cents. My brothers would receive money, too. We would take the money and spend it all in the same day.

I had two brothers, Vincent and Leonard. Vincent is the eldest and Leonard is the youngest, which puts me in the middle. We would spend ten cents for the movies; bus fare was five cents each way, which left five cents for candy. Usually, we would walk the five miles to the theater, just to keep the ten cents to buy extra candy. For a nickel, I could buy candy that weighed a half-pound. We bought a little of everything at the candy counter and ate until we were ready to burst. The movies would last five hours, with two main features, two serials (like the Lone Ranger), cartoons, and

Pathe News, all for ten cents. When we came home too full to eat dinner, Mother would be upset.

People are always complaining about school classes being overcrowded. When I went to school, twenty to thirty students per class was the norm. But when I was in the first grade, we were integrated with the kindergarten children—sixty students in one classroom. It was a small Catholic school, with only eight classrooms—that is all it could accommodate due to shortage of funds. Each class was crowded, but we still received a good education because the nuns were strict and did not take sass. To this day, I wonder how the nuns did not have nervous breakdowns. One nun, Sister Patrick, had to put up with sixty five- and six-year-olds—I think that was a great accomplishment.

I remember how my siblings and I kept busy in our spare time when we were kids—we would make our own toys. One toy was made by getting an old wooden box and short two-by-four boards, and nailing the boards to the box. Then, we would look for discarded roller-skate wheels to put under the two-by-fours so we could ride in the box. It was not a smooth ride because the wheels were made from hard steel. To make it more luxurious-looking, we would nail an empty tin can to the front of the unit and place a candle in it for night riding.

During the summer my family would go to my grandfather's farm in Flemington, New Jersey. A farmer in the area had arranged with my grandfather to plant tomatoes on some of my grandfather's acreage. In August, the farmer was looking for laborers to pick the tomatoes. Two older boys from the neighboring farm already had agreed to the job, and the farmer asked me if I also wanted to work.

I said, "Okay. How much are you paying an hour?" The price was thirty-five cents per hour—remember, it was 1935, in the middle of the Depression. I would have taken the job for twenty-five cents an hour.

I worked for about an hour one day—it was about ninety-five degrees, but the high humidity made it feel much hotter. Then, my mother came marching out with a large gallon of cold water. I said, "Thanks, Mom, for bringing the water."

She said, "This water is for the two boys and the farmer. Are you crazy, working in this heat?"

I said, "I want to make some money."

She told me, "Do you want to get sunstroke? Get to the house immediately."

I said, "Wait—I did not get paid yet."

The farmer came over and gave me thirty-five cents. (When I think back, he had to struggle to get fifty cents for a bushel of tomatoes.)

I said, "Mom, why did you make me leave?"

She said, "You looked like you were melting in the heat. I looked out from the window and saw you boys sweltering in the sun. That is why I brought cold water for the farmer and the boys."

I pretended that I was angry that she'd made me stop working, but to tell the truth, I was glad she came to get me. People were so desperate for money that they would take any kind of job. I wanted the money to buy candy and ice cream. Parents did not spoil their children in those days, even if they could afford to give them goodies.

Living through the Depression is ingrained in my brain. I remember when homes for the middle-class and wealthy did not have oil burners yet. Those who were fortunate had coal stoves in their basements for heating water. The poorer class had cold-water "flats," as they were called—no warm water in the homes. Some of my cousins who lived in a cold-water flat had only wood-burning stoves in their kitchens. They had no hot water to take a bath or shower unless they heated kettles of water on the kitchen stove. My cousins had to go to public bathhouses to take a shower. I would invite them to my house to take a shower or bath, but they would decline; they would feel embarrassed.

I was lucky to have a warm house, and I still remember the coal man. He would pull his truck in front our house. He had a chute on the back of the truck from which he would fill a canvas container with arm straps with the coal. He would then walk to the side of the house, where there were cellar windows that had openings to the coal bins. He had to carry at least fifty pounds of coal on his back each time and had to deliver one ton of coal before he was finished. After the coal burned down to ash, it was my job to carry out the ashes from the basement and put them in ash cans. In 1936, though, a miracle happened: an oil burner was installed to heat our home—no more ashes to be carried. Still, I think of that poor coal man who carried that coal for quite a few years. He made about ten dollars per week.

I remember when my older brother, Vince, bought a car from one of our neighborhood fellows for twenty dollars. It was a 1930 Willys-Knight that was ready for the junk heap. One hot summer day after he got his car, my brother told a couple of fellows and me, "Let's take a ride to Eagle Rock Mountain." The ride was about a mile and half long, all uphill. Chugging along, the car overheated and began to steam and shoot smoke from the radiator directly up into the air. My brother stopped the car and told me to go to the nearest house to ask the people for some water.

I rang the bell, and a nice lady answered. She asked, "What can I do for you, son?"

I asked if I could have some water. She immediately went into the house and returned with a glass of water.

I said, "Thank you, but I need more water for our car—it's overheating." I drank the water she'd given me, though, because I was hot and thirsty. (Remember, there was no air conditioning in cars in those days.)

She returned with a bucket of water. I thanked her several times for her hospitality. We waited a while for the car engine to cool down before we put the water into the radiator. We decided that we had better turn around because we still had about a half a mile to go, all uphill. So we turned around and, heading down this steep hill, the brakes failed to slow us down. My brother had his foot on the brake pedal all the way, but the car would not slow down. His best friend, Danny, was pulling on the emergency brake to no avail.

At the foot of this hill were two arched brick walls. In front of the walls, there were there were thick hedges. We were all screaming at Vince to crash into the hedges. The hedges were about six feet deep in front of the wall. We crashed into the hedges and hit the wall. We were traveling so fast that the car crushed the hedges and just about broke through part of the wall. The front bumper fell off, and one of the wheels was bent. Luckily, none of us was hurt, but we were darn scared. The car's body was light and that saved us from going through the wall. If we hadn't gone into the hedges and instead had gone out on the busy road, we would definitely have been hurt or killed.

The car was a total loss, although it had only cost twenty dollars. And of course, we had to walk all the way home.

In another one of his escapades, my brother bought a 1929 Auburn—a popular car of its time—for twenty-five dollars. He had a part-time job, working for Western Union. I think he was making about seven dollars a week. Whenever he had enough money, he would buy these relics. This time, he paid for the car but did not have money for license plates, so he borrowed license plates from a friend. As he was driving the car in a local park, a policeman stopped him because the car was burning more oil than gas—his car polluted the entire park with smoke emissions. I remember that the police questioned him about his license plates. He was fortunate that when the officer looked at his driver's license he noticed that his last name was the same as that of the chief of police. He asked my brother if there was any relation, and my brother explained that the chief was my dad's first cousin. The officer let him go without a summons. Politics as usual.

Much earlier in life, when he was about eight years old, his friend Danny, who had an active imagination, decided to dig a tunnel to China. Danny must have read or seen a photo about China and convinced Vince to help him. They started by pounding the basement wall in Dan's house. Two days later his older brother discovered the mess they had made in the basement wall.

"What are you boys trying to do?" he asked them.

"We want to make a tunnel to China," they answered.

Dan's older brother gave them a stern warning about not continuing to smash the wall. He told them that China was more than eight thousand miles away—they could dig for the rest of their lives and still not make it.

I remember seeing the hole in the concrete wall. After two days of pounding the wall with a sledge hammer, they had advanced only about ten inches.

In 1936, I was eleven years old, and Franklin Roosevelt defeated Alfred M. Landon to be reelected president of the United

States. The Great Depression continued, however, and our chief entertainments were still free ones. For example, my friends and I would play baseball or touch football in the city streets of our neighborhood. As I mentioned, there were not many cars in the streets in those days; in fact, on our block there were only three cars, and my family owned one of them, so there was plenty of room to throw the ball around.

I will never forget the day we decided to play ball two blocks away from our neighborhood, by our friend Jimmy's house, because his parents wanted to keep an eye on him. Jimmy was the only Irish kid and the rest of the group were Italian Americans. Fifteen minutes into the game, a police car arrived. The officers said to us, "You *Wops* get back to your own neighborhood!" Well, that was the first time I encountered discrimination. I went home very dismayed. I asked my parents what did the officer meant by "Wops," and my parents said that he had just showed his ignorance by using that term. They explained to me that the immigration agents labeled foreigners that came to America without papers as "WOP." WOP simply meant "without papers." This applied not only to Italians but to everyone entering the country without documentation. For some unknown reason, the term "Wop" became a discriminatory label for Italian Americans.

The second time that I encountered discrimination was at school a year later. Our school was composed of an even ratio of Italians and Irish. Every nun had her favorite student, and I was Sister Emanuel's favorite because I got excellent marks. I was also one of the best baseball players and track runners, and I was always the top fund-raiser. When the church would sell "chance books" to raise funds, the average student would sell enough chances to complete two books, which brought in two dollars. America was still going through the Depression, so donations were difficult to get. Well, I had an advantage because I would go with my dad to his workplace and sell to his customers. A customer often would buy an entire book of chances because he figured that my dad would give him a better wholesale price on the merchandise. One time, I sold twenty-five books (and raised twenty-five dollars). I was the star of the money-raisers. The school and church were dependent on donations, so this was a big deal.

All in all, I figured that I was guaranteed a spot as a traffic patrol guard, an honor that all us kids wanted. I thought that I would be given the position of chief patrol officer because I was the best money-raiser and a star athlete. When the time came to award the badges, however, the chief's badge was given to Bill Murphy, and I was given the assistant chief's badge. I went to talk to Sister Emanuel and argued that Bill did not play ball, track, or any sports. She gave me an explanation that I will never forget: A donor, who was Irish, had given one hundred dollars to the church with the stipulation that they give the chief's patrol badge to Bill Murphy, who, incidentally, was also Irish. I later told Bill that he had beat me purely by politics. Bill and I were friendly to each other so he wasn't offended by the remark. But I never forgot that lesson about politics. That happened over sixty-seven years ago.

After I graduated from grammar school, I wanted to go to my brother's Catholic high school because they had great athletic teams. My parents told me that I could not go because they were unable to pay the tuition—it was $250 a year. Instead, I went to a public high school and tried out for the freshman football team. When I showed up, guys who were all tall and weighed at least 150 pounds surrounded me. I was five foot five and a half inches tall and weighed one hundred pounds soaking wet. The coach took one look at me and told me to come back in three years.

"I can outrun all those overgrown kids," I insisted.

He looked at me again and said, "Come back in three years."

That was the end of my football career.

In high school, I hung out with a group of about a half a dozen young fellows. Our meeting spot was by the large mail storage box on the corner of Fifteenth Street. There was a candy store right there on the corner. The shop owner, Mrs. Shearer, used to sell charlotte russes for three cents. Once, Bill, the neighborhood bad boy, bought one and said that the whipped cream filling was sour. Mrs. Shearer, the store owner, refused to give him his three cents back because he had devoured over half of it. He had a bad reputation, so she did not believe him. To get even, he smeared her front glass window with the rest of the whipped cream. Unknown to us, Mrs. Shearer had called the Bloomfield Police. Within minutes a patrol car showed up and put five of us in the back seat. Of course, Bill ran away without telling us that Mrs. Shearer had called the police. We tried to explain to the police that we had nothing to do with the window episode, but we also refused to say who was responsible. We were ushered into City Hall and jail. When they closed the jail door, it was quite frightening. We all agreed not to squeal on Bill, not that he didn't deserve it. We had our own "Cosa Nostra"—our code of honor.

Then, a policeman came and told us we had to call our parents and tell them that we were scheduled to appear before the judge; our parents were required to come to night court. Well, in those days, most parents would believe their kids were guilty before the kids could defend themselves. I called my dad and told him to come to the night court. The judge had us line up in front of the bench. We tried to explain to the judge that we were innocent, but the judge said that if we were not guilty then we should name the person who had done the deed. None of us wanted to be the informant.

Ultimately, the judge let us go free but with the warning that if anything ever happened again, he would keep us in jail. He knew we would get some kind of punishment from our parents, but when I told my dad what happened, he understood. He knew Bill was a troublemaker with a bad reputation.

Later on, Bill was in more trouble with the law. There was a city stadium near our neighborhood. Once a week, there would be a concert at the stadium in the evening. Cars would have to park along the city streets because there was very limited parking at the stadium. One evening, the police came knocking on our door and asked us if we had seen anyone running on our block. A woman had told the police that she'd seen a person run toward our block with stolen merchandise in his hand—someone had been stealing things out of the parked cars.

Bill lived on our block. When I heard the conversation, I knew the culprit was Bill. The week previous, Bill had been wearing sunglasses and showing off his new flashlight, along with other items. The next time I saw Bill, I told him that he had better stop stealing before he gets arrested because the police will have to put him in jail. I also warned him that if his older brother found out what he was doing, there really would be hell to pay.

Bill just shrugged it off. A few years later, he was caught robbing a store at gunpoint. He was put away for a couple of years. I could not understand his actions. He had two older brothers who were nice people and who would mind their own business. They had decent jobs and went to work every day. Bill's father had died before he was born and his mother was an invalid, so Bill had very little discipline. I guess that is why he went out of control.

I still remember that as teenagers, my friends and I would try to impress the opposite sex. I always felt self-conscious about my height, so I always made up for it with my outgoing personality. I had a driver's license when I was sixteen. I was able to obtain a license at that age instead of waiting until seventeen, which was the official requirement in New Jersey at the time, because I accompanied my uncle and grandfather to White Sulfur Springs, West Virginia. My grandfather's doctor had recommended sulfur baths for his health. When I heard you could obtain a driver's license at sixteen in West Virginia, I asked my uncle to accompany me to the DMV. I took the test and passed. Naturally I was thrilled to accomplish something that my peers had to wait for.   Plus, I had the advantage over the other fellows because I could borrow my dad's car.

A fellow was considered really something if he could date a girl and drive to her home. Some of the fellows were jealous of me because I could use my dad's car; not too many families could afford a car. My dad would retire early because he had to wake up at 2:00 AM. He had to keep terrible hours, but that was the nature of the import wholesale produce business. My mother did not drive, and by this time, my older brother, Vince, was in the U.S. Army, so the car was available every weekday evening. If my mother had to go somewhere, I would accommodate her. Otherwise, I had the freedom to use this transportation. Fuel was economical then—fifteen cents per gallon.

When I took a girl to a place that would serve drinks to minors, we would have a ball. Soft drinks were ten cents and alcoholic drinks were twenty-five cents. Some of these owners knew we were underage and made sure we were allowed only two drinks. They would not have any trouble with me because after one strong drink, I'd had enough. (To this day, I do not care for alcoholic drinks. Occasionally, I will drink a glass of wine.)

We all had temptations when we were young. When you have parents who teach you right from wrong and are strict, though, you grow up the rest of your life on the right road. Most of the fellows I grew up with were very successful in life. We would need every bit of strength to face the great war that was coming our way.

Chapter 2

World War II

In 1940, Franklin D. Roosevelt was elected to his third term as United States president. He told Americans that our boys would never be sent overseas, but behind the scenes, he was working all kinds of deals with Winston Churchill. Americans were isolationists and didn't want any part of the war in Europe. During this time, Roosevelt was also putting sanctions on Japan. The United States' tactic was to intimidate Japan and hope that Germany would sink one of our ships that carried supplies to England. Sinking a U.S. ship would give FDR a reason to start a war.

Japan noticed that Germany was winning the war, so it wanted to get aggressive, figuring that the United States was ill prepared. Meanwhile, our president was trying to get America into the war. He knew that if the dictators won the war in Europe, they would eventually attack us. Roosevelt figured that the best way to do that was to force the Japanese to attack us, because the American public would not accept our attacking another country. Japan had almost all of 1941 to figure out what to do.

When I went into the navy, there was no question in my mind why we were fighting. The only thing that bothered me was why our president, Franklin D. Roosevelt, lied to us, saying that our boys would never be sent overseas, when all the while, he was scheming to get us into the war. Why not tell the American public the truth? Did he think we were stupid?

I was only seventeen years old when we were aiding England with the Lend-Lease program, sending them ships, tanks, etc. America had to find a way to defeat the dictators and to free all the people in concentrations camps.

Vince had joined the army by then. He told me that some soldiers had to train with broomsticks in Fort Dix, New Jersey, because whatever supplies the army had were secretly being sent to England.

I was in school at this time, but I watched the events closely. Japan sent two diplomats to try to negotiate a deal in Washington. The Japanese knew that our president would not make any concessions, so they decided to attack Pearl Harbor. I knew we had to get into the war sooner or later, but I did not agree with the method—our soldiers and sailors were not forewarned. Our commanders knew that Japan had planes approaching the outer islands of Hawaii. The president and others ignored the warning. The command was conveniently missing in Pearl Harbor. Why were all our battleships moved from San Diego to Pearl Harbor? To make it easier for Japan to Attack? I will never forgive President Roosevelt for not giving those poor sailors a warning so that they could at least try to defend themselves. As a result, over two thousand sailors were killed on the battleship *Arizona*, in addition to the other army and navy personnel on land. The following day, President Roosevelt beamed in front of Congress, saying, "This is a day that will live in infamy." In my mind, the way those sailors died will live in infamy. The United States was unprepared for the attack. In the meantime, boys were being drafted at a quickening pace. My brother was about to be shipped overseas, and, ultimately, he went with General Patton's Third Army.

Civilian life in the United States consisted of rationing—everything was rationed, from gas to meat. My friend Danny was deferred from the draft for health reasons and worked for General Electric. He worked from 7:00 AM to 7:00 PM, seven days a week. When he showed me his first paycheck for ninety dollars, we both stared at it for over half an hour. I finally said to him, "Maybe the Depression is over."

I was still in school, but Dad's business was not doing well because German U-boats were sinking cargo ships off the East

Coast nearly every day. My dad's business depended on imports from tropical countries, and eventually, he had to close his business because he could not receive any merchandise. Things were pretty tight for us, and I had to look elsewhere for employment. Eventually, I obtained a job in the summer, delivering bread in Staten Island, New York. My employer instructed me not to leave any bread at a certain customer's house on the route because she had bills that were past due. When I arrived at her house and asked for payment, the woman told me that she didn't have the money. I looked inside and saw five young children (I guessed their ages to be from about five years old down to one year old). I asked her where her husband was, and she replied that he had been dead for six months. I couldn't understand how she could survive. She reluctantly explained that she received city relief—the government paid her rent of eighteen dollars a month but nothing more. Whenever possible, she took in wet laundry for ironing, at three dollars a load. I felt sorry for her. I went back to my delivery truck and retrieved the last six loaves of bread and gave it to the woman. I told her to forget her bill, that I would be giving her free bread all summer, as long as I was on the route.

When I arrived back in New Jersey, I told my employer what I had done and that he could take the cost of the bread out of my pay. He said he would do so, but when payday came around, he had not deducted a single cent. He made me feel good; he figured I had done a good deed.

During this period, my dad's health was failing and the rent was due. He had one more payment of $29.30 on a 1940 Packard that had cost $1,040. He would not ask my mother's father for any more help. My brother was getting thirty dollars a month from the army, which was barely enough to get by. I asked my other grandfather—my dad's father—for money, and he gave me a check for the amount of the car payment. I told him I would pay him as soon I could, which I did.

My brother Vince had a lifelong friend, Dan—he was also my friend; I knew him for seventy-five years before he passed away in 2006. He was quite a guy. He was the first president of our athletic and social club. He organized our football and baseball teams. The teams were very successful and were the talk of the city. He kept the teams together and also managed to keep their morale up at all times. He made sure they had their equipment, even though money was still scarce. I was the team treasurer and had to collect the dues—two dollars every month from each member—to pay the rent on the store we leased for our meetings. Although we had just come out the Depression, money was still tight. I had to pull hard on some of the guys for monthly dues. We couldn't downsize though, as we were close to one hundred members and needed space . We'd started at our homes for meetings but had long since outgrown them.

Out of our one hundred members, ninety-five had been in the military. Some volunteered—like my brother Vince in 1940—and others were drafted, including me. Dan had been rejected from the military because he had arthritis.

He was working twelve hours a day, seven days a week, yet he managed to send letters to all of us during that four-year period that we were in the military. Dan sent us a monthly newsletter, too, to let us know what was happening back home, even though it would take three months before we would receive it, due to the military censors.

Dan had not been able to go to college because his family could not afford to pay the cost. Over the next ten years, he worked different jobs. Once, he met a character who talked him into getting a truck and going into the milk business. Milk was delivered to the homes in those days. He stayed in the business for several years and managed to eke out a living—he worked very hard, had early hours, and faced cold weather. and many other problems.

Later on, after WWII, that same character who had talked Dan into the milk business told him that he saw a great opportunity to buy into the jukebox business. The government was cracking down on the shady people in that business at that time. This character told Dan that if they could put up ten thousand dollars between them as a down payment, they could buy certain locations for seventy thousand dollars. That included sixty locations with jukeboxes, pool tables, pinball machines, etc. The terms for payment were very lenient. Shady characters were anxious to disengage themselves from the business because they were under scrutiny by the government. Dan came to my home to get my advice on the matter. I told him that I thought it was a great idea. My wife, Marge, said, "Do you want to be a milkman all your life?" We loaned him some money, and my brother Vince gave him some also. He promised to pay us back as soon as he could. About nine months went by before I saw Dan again, and I asked him, "How are you doing in the business?"

In a sad tone, he said, "I am just about making a living. We have to pay two thousand dollars a month to the original owners."

I said, "So what? You have sixty locations with all kinds of equipment, plus protection from the characters who sold you the business. You should be making plenty of money now. I am not telling you this so that you will pay back the money that Vince and I loaned you. There is something wrong, and I think I know what it is. I only met your partner twice, but he never impressed me as being honest. I did not trust him, but I never mentioned it to you. Does he have keys to all the machines in every location? If he does, you are very vulnerable to being cheated."

Dan responded, "Yes, he does."

I said, "I think he is stealing."

"Maybe you are right," he agreed, "because a couple of the tavern owners have been complaining to me that customers have been playing with the equipment, but the money does not show."

A couple weeks went by, and then Danny called me, saying he had something to tell me. He said, "You know the neighborhood tavern, Al's Bar & Grill? Every Sunday morning, when the maintenance man is cleaning, my so-called partner comes in and takes money from all the machines that I am supposed to collect from. That makes me look dishonest, when I am innocent."

Dan decided to ask the tavern owner if he would hide behind the bar the next Sunday, and the tavern owner agreed. Sure enough—he saw Dan's partner come in and take money out of the machines. The tavern owner was upset, and Dan's partner—the thief —left the premises, scared. Later, Dan called him and told him, "Meet me tomorrow, and we will go to the lawyer's office and split this route in two."

I told him that he should have turned his partner over to the people from whom he bought the business—they would have taken care of him, Mafia-style. But Dan did not want to get into trouble; he just wanted to break clean from the partner. He went on to expand the business and eventually brought in his sons. They are still operating the business today. By the way, thirty days after he broke from his sneaky partner, he paid back my brother and me the money we had loaned him.

I still miss him. We would talk to each other every other week. He would tell me what was happening in New Jersey, and I would tell him about California, where I had moved. The few members from the old club that are still alive still remember him because he kept in contact with them, even when we all became senior citizens. Of the one hundred original members, I believe there may be about a half a dozen who are still with us. I communicate once in a while with a couple of the old boys.

Dan was a workaholic; his only vacation was in 1942, with me, in Long Branch, New Jersey. We spent only a weekend, and he was anxious to go to back to work. It was midsummer—the weather was nice and warm; the ocean water was warm.

I said, "Let's stay and enjoy ourselves," but he would not hear of it. Believe it or not, that was his first and last vacation in sixty years. I think that was because the Depression never left him. He had the reputation of being a miser, and I can vouch for that. I picked up many checks that he could have. We both could afford to pay, but he hated to part with his money. I think he had the fear of another depression coming.

The following year, the German subs were busy sinking our merchant ships in the North Atlantic that the sea lanes were left open on the East Coast. This allowed my dad to reopen his business, and he started importing produce again. I had just finished school and was about to be drafted. I tried to get an extension on my draft status by reporting to the draft board that my dad needed my help to run the business; that without me, he would have only my fourteen-year-old brother at home. The draft board rejected my excuse, and I was immediately drafted.

I was sent in front of the military board, which decided to send me to the Marines. I argued that with my physical stature, I wouldn't make a good Marine. I told them that I was barely over a hundred pounds and only five foot five. It wouldn't be possible for me to carry a fifty-pound pack on my back or go on a twenty-mile hike. The recruiter took another look at me, then passed me up. The board decided to put me in the navy, which was where I wanted to go in the first place. I was put on a train with all of the other inductees and sent to Newport, Rhode Island, for boot camp training. I received the usual medical shots and physical. When waiting in line, other sailors

who had their shots would tease the guys to watch out for the square needle.

Later, I was asked what job I would be interested in, and I answered that I wanted to study intercommunications. Instead, they sent me to electrician's school, which was all theory study. The rumor was that anyone who failed would be sent to Pier 92 in New York City—that was where all the cargo ships left for the Murmansk Route in the North Atlantic on their way to Russia. The Merchant Marines on those ships received a bonus of five thousand dollars if they arrived safely in Russia, and the navy sailors who manned the guns on the same ship were paid sixty-two dollars per month. The drawback was that, on average, only one out of three ships actually made it. After I heard this, I studied my butt off and graduated with a 4.0 average. It was not that I was chicken; let's just say that I was careful. Believe it or not, I was asked what ship I wanted to serve on. I came from New Jersey so I chose the battleship *Missouri* because it had been constructed in Brooklyn, New York, which was relatively close to home. There must have been one thousand sailors assigned to destroyers, aircraft carriers, cruisers, submarines, and battleships. I was sweating it out because my last name began with "S," and they were going in alphabetical order. I ended up being the last one called for the *Missouri*.

I was then shipped to Brooklyn, New York, where the *Missouri* was being fitted with guns and would not to be commissioned for another thirty days. I was then sent to Fire Control School in Philadelphia, Pennsylvania, and trained for three weeks before being shipped back to Brooklyn.

The week after returning, the ship was commissioned. Margaret Truman, the vice president's daughter, smashed the champagne into the bow of the ship before it was sent on its maiden voyage. It was January 1944. The ship immediately went on its shakedown cruise to Cuba and Trinidad—this was to correct any faults with the ship. It passed with flying colors. Now, I was on my way to the Pacific. It took several days to finally reach the Panama Canal. The Panama Canal dry docks are 110 feet wide, and the *Missouri* was 108 feet wide. It was a tight squeeze, but the ship made it through okay and headed to San Francisco, where it was docked for three weeks to board ammunition, oil, and cargo. Then we headed for Pearl Harbor and spent another week loading food. Just to give an idea of the amounts, there were three freight cars of just spaghetti—the ship had over one thousand Italian Americans aboard. The cooks massacred the pasta, and the gravy was watery with raw tomatoes—not like Mama would make it. At sea, I learned to overlook many things; after all, America was at war. After loading the supplies, we sailed to the war zone in the Pacific.

Then everything became very serious.

I was assigned to the electrical control board that was located in Engine Room Number 2. My job was to cut into alternate power in the event of a power failure. The power was very important because it controlled the guns for firepower. Each watch was very stressful; it consisted of four hours on and four hours off while in the battle zone. But the shifts didn't bother me as much as the unbearable heat. It was always 90 to 110 degrees in there. I was a little over 110 pounds when I started, and I shrank down to 100 pounds, even. There were salt pills by the drinking fountain but that didn't help very much. Eventually, I complained to my chief petty officer and asked for a reassignment. I was a petty officer and was eligible for a change. He said he would think about it, but I never heard another word until an incident occurred that I could hold over his head. Our lieutenant commander was known for squeezing himself between the bilge plates and steam generators; he would shut the power off without notice. The person on the control board would need to immediately turn on the alternate power or the ship would be without firepower. I was already aware that he came between the hours of midnight and four in the morning. He was nicknamed "Turkey Neck" because he was able to squeeze his head between the small spaces of the bilge plates. One night, I was on the early morning watch, and at about 1:00 AM, my chief came in the engine room to speak with me. He sat down about ten feet from where I was seated. There was a large exhaust fan that brought air in from the outside, which made a deafening noise, but the constant humming also had a hypnotic effect. As a result of the heat and noise, the chief eventually fell asleep. During the course of my shift, I saw the lieutenant commander slip his skinny head and body through the bilges, and just as he pulled the switch, I immediately turned on the alternate power. The chief awoke suddenly because the fan noise had stopped and started up again. The lieutenant commander came to our platform and congratulated the chief for his quick reaction in immediately getting the power restored. If the lieutenant commander knew that the chief had been asleep, he would have put him on report and sent him to the brig (jail). He could have received ten years in the military jail back in the United States. The navy was very strict when it came to sleeping on duty. I said to the chief, "I saved your butt, and you received the credit. I want to get out of this hot box as soon as possible." Within three days I was transferred to intercommunications and an air-conditioned workroom. The change in temperature made me lose my voice for a few days. I went from working in 100 degrees to 65 degrees, but I loved it. I thanked the chief for the transfer, and he told me to keep my mouth shut about what had happened.

In January of 1945, we encountered our first kamikaze planes near Iwo Jima. Admiral Halsey was assigned to the *Missouri*. We were the flagship for the 38th Fleet. I remember the day when all hell broke loose and dozens of kamikaze planes were heading to attack the entire fleet. After the battle was over, Admiral Halsey wanted to know how many planes our guns had shot down and how many total were destroyed. The answer was that three or four had been shot down, and ten or eleven were destroyed. Halsey ordered us to paint ten Japanese flags on our bridge, one for each plane. We were only entitled to paint one for each plane that was destroyed, but Halsey was the boss, so ten Japanese flags were painted on our bridge.

We headed onward to Iwo Jima to join the rest of the battleships

that were bombarding the island. Our ships fired at the island in twelve-hour shifts, and this lasted continuously for two days. For many of us, the fillings in our teeth fell out due to the vibrations of the sixteen-inch guns. In the meantime, the Japanese were entrenched in their caves, and our sixteen-inch shells only made foxholes for our marines. The first day of the ground attack, nineteen thousand Marines were wounded or killed. The only way the Marines could root out the Japanese from the caves was to use flamethrowers directed inside the caves. The Marines had to climb uphill to reach the caves, which resulted in many casualties. I am not trying to be an "armchair general," but to invade a small island (not even two miles by four miles wide) with a mountain from which to look down at our Marines was a blunder.

Only two months later, we invaded Okinawa, which had a sixty-five-mile coastline. This made it much easier to find a soft spot to invade. We attacked Okinawa, and there were no casualties on the beach but the fighting was ferocious inland. The Japanese threw all of the kamikazes at our fleet. I will never forget it. The date was March 19, 1945. A suicide plane was headed for our ship.

Luckily, our five-inch guns hit the bomb carrier, and the bomb dropped into the ocean, just inches from the ship. The plane, however, crashed into our ship and blew up. I was on my general quarters station on deck for fire control, and I witnessed everything that took place. The pilot was thrown from the plane; both of his legs were blown off, and he died instantly. He looked much younger than eighteen years old, which meant that the enemy was desperate. Their entire air force was out there. They hit and sunk 117 ships in the battle. Nineteen were battleships; none of those was sunk.

Our ship headed for northern Japan, where we started to shell factories from about five miles offshore. We saw smokestacks falling down due to the shelling. Not one plane tried to attack our ship. To invade the Japanese mainland would be very costly. The Japanese were very fanatical people at that time and would have fought to the last man because they were taught that it was very shameful to surrender. Our command sent out peace feelers but the Japanese refused.

Meantime, President Roosevelt died in April 1945. He never was able to see the European or Japanese fighting come to an end. Vice President Harry S. Truman succeeded Roosevelt. I knew the new president's nephew John Truman from serving aboard the *Missouri*. I had a higher rank than he did, and I would tease him and say that if I were the president's nephew, I would be the captain of this ship. He would just laugh it off. He was a regular, nice person.

We retreated to a South Pacific island called Ulithi. Most of the fleet was there for rest. Every sailor was given two cans of beer or two bottles of Coca-Cola. There must have been fifty thousand sailors on this little island, which was uninhabited. There were thousands of craps games going on at once. We were allowed only four hours liberty before having to return to our ships.

Several months passed without any change until, at the beginning of August, we got a news flash: an atomic bomb landed on Hiroshima. The Japanese still did not capitulate. Several days later, the United States hit the city of Nagasaki with the second bomb. The chaplain on our ship complained that the second bomb hit the only Catholic city in Japan. History proved that they would not have surrendered if they thought we had only one bomb. This second bomb had them guessing. The truth is that there were only two. Finally, the Japanese surrendered, which saved lives on both sides.

The historic arguments between General McArthur and Admiral Nimitz started after the bombing. The general wanted the peace terms signed in Manila, Philippines. Nimitz wanted the navy to have a say. History does not mention this and few, if any, historians know about it, but I was in intercommunications and had friends in the radio shack. In those days, messages would come through Teletype. After a week of deliberation, a Teletype came in, and the decision was that the peace terms would be held on the battleship *Missouri*. We were all elated. Once again, the decision was due to politics. President Truman was from Missouri. Why not the Mighty MO? We were all jockeying for spots to get a view of the proceedings. I maneuvered a ringside view and saw it all.

In October 1944, when General MacArthur was about to invade the Philippines, the Japanese Navy was going to confront his landing. Admiral Halsey wanted to assist MacArthur, and he ordered us and the 38th Fleet to head for the Philippines, disregarding a warning that a typhoon was heading in our direction. We had to endure two days of tremendous, violent waves. Three of our destroyers were sunk due to the storm. All the crews of those three ships were lost. There were rumors that the top officer was going to be reprimanded for his actions or that there would be a court-martial, but this never came about.

After the Japanese surrendered, we arrived in Pearl Harbor, took on supplies, and headed for San Francisco. We docked there for a week. The military was discharging qualified sailors who lived in the western part of the country. Married men had seniority and were discharged first. I was only twenty-one at the time and not married, so I had to wait my turn. Afterward, the ship proceeded to Newport News, Virginia, and then on to Brooklyn, our home port. We were given ten days liberty, and I was reunited with my family

I tried to make up for the three years that I'd missed with my girlfriends. I came back to find that some of them were married, so they were off limits. My liberty flew by. As usual, nothing new.

USS Missouri Reunion in Colorado

After Pearl Harbor a few additional ships were damaged or sunk in the Pacific Ocean. I remember when the aircraft carrier USS *Franklin* was hit by a Japanese suicide plane in the Pacific Ocean. Our ship, the USS *Missouri*, was close by. We were summoned to help extinguish the fire. I saw sights then that I will never forget. There were 724 sailors killed aboard that ship and 265 wounded. Their bodies were smeared against the ship's bulkheads. It was the most upsetting sight anyone could witness. Those poor sailors did not have a chance, with that aviation fuel igniting and spreading amidships. It was pathetic to see all these young sailors burned to death, their bodies torn apart all over the ship, upper and lower decks. They gave their lives to protect everyone's freedom, the youth of the country. The ship survived, but the propellers were jammed, so it was towed backwards by the USS *Pittsburgh* to Pearl Harbor and then on its own power to New York. They had a seventh war bond drive for the memory of the sailors who were killed.

My cousin survived because he was in the aft (back end) of the ship. Our ship, the USS *Missouri*, was alongside the *Franklin*. The target could have been our ship. Several months later, we were hit buy a Japanese plane, but the damage was not as bad as the *Franklin*'s.

I still get emotional when I think about those attacks. The poor sailors did not have a chance to survive. I found some comfort in knowing there would be a seventh war bond drive for the memory of the sailors who perished in that terrible disaster aboard the *Franklin*. God bless them. They gave their lives to protect everyone's freedom.

There were in the military when I was discriminated against when I said I was an Italian American. The first thing I would hear is, "Are you in the Mafia?" Aboard ship, there was a twenty-year service man—all brawn, no brains. When I came off a 4:00 AM watch at 7:00 AM, he would wake me with "Wop ... Dago ... it is time for your watch." We had quite a few Italian Americans in our compartment who had fear of this redneck. He hated Italians, Negroes—anyone who was different from him. I would tell the others not to be afraid. I told that 250-pound bully that if he called me Wop or any other term again, I would report him to the lieutenant commander. From that day on, he ceased calling any of us derogatory names. I still remember my shipmate, Donahue, another twenty-year man, congratulating me for putting the bully in his place. Also, I remember climbing up the ladder compartment to leave the ship when I was discharged. Four African Americans were waiting to descend to our compartment. The bully was still there. I turned and said to the bully, "I hope you have a fine time with the new boys." His face became flushed; he knew what I meant. I knew how he hated Negroes. I left the ship laughing—the government had just passed a law banning discrimination in service.

The day after we docked in Brooklyn, the public was allowed to view the ship. The first guests were President Truman, his wife, and his daughter, plus all the dignitaries from all over the country. It reminded me of when we were in San Francisco. There were many movie stars who would come aboard, like Clark Gable and Dick Powell. I believe every person in New York City came to see the ship—it was the talk of the country. Everyone wanted to see the plaque of the peace terms that was imbedded in the deck; it had the date inscribed—9/2/45—when the peace terms were signed. It also had symbols of General MacArthur, Admiral Nimitz, and Admiral Halsey. I still have medallions at home that were made to commemorate the event.

At the end of liberty, it was back to the grind. It was now December 1945, and the rumor was that the ship was scheduled to stay in the Brooklyn Navy Yard for another two months. It didn't matter to me; I just wanted to figure a way to get discharged. The military discharged men according to a point system, and I was only one-quarter of a point short. A buddy of mine was already approved to get discharged, and he told me to get his old job of driving the captain around town. He said to talk to a Lt. Ramsey and explain to him that I knew the area very well. The driver's job was scheduled as one day on and two days off. I ended up getting the job, and the captain was a great guy. He had an apartment on East Ninety-second Street. His wife was a lovely woman—warm and friendly. I would drive them to restaurants downtown; then afterwards, back to his residence to drop off his wife. The captain would have to return to the ship at the end of the evening.

One day during the Christmas season, the captain asked me to drive him and his wife to Grand Central Station, where they were taking a train to Washington DC. He said that they would be gone eleven days and to pick them up when they returned. He also instructed me to not allow anyone to use his naval car during his absence. After wishing him and his wife happy holidays, I took off for New Jersey. I knew there was a dance at the Elks Club, and I did not want to get there too late—I wanted to be there before all the girls were taken. I had the car going seventy miles per hour on the Pulaski Highway in a fifty-mile-an-hour zone, when all of a sudden I heard sirens, and a policeman told me to pull aside. He asked me why I was driving at such a high speed. I lied and said that the captain of USS *Missouri* was arriving in the Newark (New Jersey) Penn Station, and I was running late. He told me to follow him. He had his sirens blowing and red lights glaring as he escorted me directly to the station. I was hoping that he wouldn't insist on coming into the station; otherwise, I would be a goner when he found out I'd lied. I thanked him, and he gave me a salute before he pulled away with his motorcycle. That was a close one, but I got away with it because everyone was patriotic right after the war. I waited a few minutes, then headed off to the dance and flirted with the girls. The girls loved to be with men in uniform, so I did pretty well.

After a few days of driving the captain's car around, I received a call at my home from one of the other captain's drivers. (There were three of us total.) He advised me to get my butt back to the ship in a hurry, because Executive Officer Malone had been looking for the car and was raging mad. They had been calling for the captain's driver on the PA system every half hour for the past twenty-four hours. Commander Malone's car had broken down; it needed a water pump. There was a shortage of any kind of parts after the war, so it was going to be a while before it was fixed. I was definitely in real trouble. My brain was traveling at a fast pace as I tried to come up with a story—it was almost as fast as I was rushing from New Jersey to the Brooklyn Navy Yard. When I arrived at the ship, I heard my name called over the PA system: "Sorge, captain's driver, report to Commander Malone's office." When I went up the forward gangway, a young ensign asked me how long I had been in the navy. When I told him that

I had been in for three years, he told me that I should know that the enlisted men must use the aft (back) gangway. When I told him that I was the captain's driver that they were looking for, he kind of jumped and told me that I should go to Commander Malone's office immediately.

On the way there, I knew that I was going to have to make the biggest bluff of my young life. The marine standing guard in front of Malone's office announced me, and when I entered, the first thing I saw was the commander's face—a fiery Irish red from fury. He asked me, "Who gave you permission to hold the captain's car?"

I responded meekly, "The captain, sir."

He then said, "You better be telling the truth, or you will be spending a long time in the brig!"

I knew that if things went wrong, I would be sitting in the navy jail in Quantico, Virginia, for ten years or better. "In the meantime, Commander," I said, "I am at your disposal."

After he simmered down, he asked if he could use the captain's car. Now was my chance to play hero, and I told him that the captain would not object if he knew the circumstances. I then offered to take full responsibility if there was a problem. I was instructed to pick him up by five o'clock that evening. He started acting very nice to me, but if he had known the truth, he would have sent me straight to the brig.

In the evening, when I walked out to the car, there were two ensigns just standing by the car. They asked if I could take them to New York City. I told them that I was just the driver, and it would be up to Commander Malone. Surprisingly, Malone came out and agreed to give them a ride. We drove to the city, dropped off the two ensigns on Madison Avenue, and drove on to a restaurant on Sixth Avenue. Malone got out and asked me to pick him up at 11:00 PM.

I responded, "Yes, sir, I will be your driver for the next six days."

He asked me whether I wanted to take some time off, but I told him that I was responsible for the car. Anyway, I figured that the part for his car might arrive before the six days were up, which would relieve me from driving him around and still make me look good. For the next few days, I was at his beck and call, but I didn't complain. My rationale was that if he checked with the captain about my taking the car home, he might go easy on me. The water pump for his car ended up coming early, just two days before the captain returned.

I went to pick up the captain and his wife at the train station, as scheduled. I took his wife to their apartment and drove the captain back to the ship. On the way, I confessed that I had taken the car home to New Jersey, and that the commander's car had broken down, and he made me drive him around in the captain's car. The captain responded that he had not authorized me to take the car home, but that the commander could "blow his smoke out his butt." That was the second jam I had talked my way out of it within a couple of weeks.

My schedule went back to the one day on, two days off. It was an easy job, but I was getting a little impatient and wanted to get out of the navy. One night, when I was driving the captain, I asked him if he could help get me discharged. He said he would try, if it was what I really wanted. He told me that the ship was going to the Mediterranean to take the body of a UN Turkish diplomat back to Istanbul. In addition, the Cold War was starting, slowly but surely, and the military wanted some defense out in Europe. He told me that this was my chance to see Europe. The ship was scheduled to be gone for only three months, and it would not be under wartime conditions. It would basically be like a vacation. I trusted the captain; he was like a father to me. I decided to stay in the navy and head off to Turkey. I was glad that I did. It was a great trip.

Everything the captain had told me about the trip was in confidence. The crew knew we had a body aboard but did not know from what country. I felt like the cat that swallowed the canary. Two days before we arrived in Turkey, I told one of my buddies, Morris Rabkin, to buy cartons of cigarettes. The price of cigarettes was forty cents a carton out at sea. I already had my locker filled to the top. My brother, who fought with General Patton's Third Army, told me that cartons were selling for as high as a hundred dollars a carton on land. Two days later our ship arrived in Istanbul. Anchored in the bay was a Russian heavy cruiser. The Russians were trying to intimidate the Turkish population. Well, the United States would not have any of that type of harassment.

We anchored about two thousand yards away. The Russians did not allow anyone to view their ship because they were suspicious of everyone. Of course, Captain Hillenkoter allowed the public to tour the *Missouri*. For three days, thousands of people toured the Mighty MO. To show their appreciation, the locals made cigarettes with the name "Missouri" on every cigarette. That made us feel good, to see they appreciated our presence.

Next, we headed to Spain, Algiers, the Kasbah, Tangier, and Morocco. At Piraeus, Greece, I warned Morris to hold on to his cigarettes, and if he did not, then he shouldn't look to me for any handouts. Regardless of my advice, he sold all his cartons for three dollars a piece; he was all smiles. I said to him, "You are not very smart, being Jewish." I knew that the price would be higher once we hit Italy. Our next stop was Naples, Italy. As soon as we dropped anchor, two Italians came rowing out to the back of our ship. There were no language barriers because there were plenty of Italian boys from Brooklyn on our ship. Soon, there were two ropes going between the little boat and our ship. One rope had a carton of cigarettes halfway down, and the other rope was being pulled up with a fifty-dollar bill for payment. This transfer went on for fifteen minutes. I figured that if they rowed out to the ship and paid fifty dollars a carton, it must be one hundred dollars a carton on shore. The news spread all over the ship, and the ship stores were under strict orders not to sell cigarettes to anyone. Well, I was sitting pretty, with twenty cartons in my locker. My brother had made quite a bit of money selling Mickey Mouse watches to Russian soldiers. He paid one dollar for each watch at the army exchange, and the Russian soldiers paid four hundred dollars per watch. Another soldier had taken my brother to the train station in Prague, Czechoslovakia, where the transactions took place. The Russians had hundreds of dollars of American invasion money, all in hundred-dollar bills. My brother made over thirty thousand dollars selling those watches.

In Italy we were allowed to go ashore for liberty for three days. I stuffed about forty packs of cigarettes and a pound of coffee in the lining of my pea coat. I looked like the Hunchback of Notre Dame. When my buddies and I got ashore, one of the sailors said that he'd met a U.S. soldier, whom he new from back home, who told him where to get some women. He took us to a house, and we were greeted by a woman who looked war-torn. She told us in Italian that she had to pimp off her daughters to survive. The war had just ended, so food was hard to come by, and everything was sold on the black market at very high prices. The three other guys with me could not wait to see the girls. I was the only one who actually understood Italian, and I had already made up my mind that I would not touch her daughters. When she brought the girls out from behind a curtain, I saw that they were pretty but very young. The mother told me that her daughters were twelve and thirteen and a half. I asked her about her husband, and she explained that he had been killed in Africa during the war. That was it. I took out two packs of cigarettes and the coffee and gave it to her. I told the other three guys to put ten dollars each on the table. My contribution was fifty dollars—the coffee was worth twenty-five dollars and cigarettes worth twenty-five. All in all, we gave her eighty dollars. She fell on her knees and kissed my hand, crying. I ordered my friends to get out, and they had to listen to me. I was the only one with cigarettes left, so I was the boss. They all mumbled that I had done that because she was Italian. I said, "How could you have a clear conscience, having sex with young girls?" To this day, I get very emotional when I think about that incident.

The four of us were two Italians, one Irish, and one Jewish guy, but we were all Americans. I promised them that at the bars, I would pick up all the tabs. Once when we arrived at the bars, getting girls was easy. I just had to place a pack of cigarettes on the table, and the girls would come swarming at us. I told the other fellows that if they needed a pack to get girls, then I would give it to them. It felt good to be the king of the boys, all for a four-cent pack of cigarettes. At one stop, the bartender asked to buy a carton from me. I sold it to him for a hundred dollars and directions to a decent hotel. (My first thought was that in the States, cigarettes were selling for twenty cents a pack.) We were directed to a small hotel a few blocks from the bar. The hotel had only ten rooms, but it was very clean and had a shower in every room. It was also very expensive—eight dollars for two rooms. I gave the clerk two packs of cigarettes as payment, and he was very pleased. He even provided us with extra towels. These people were more impressed with cigarettes than with money. They were addicted and had to have them. I guess we were addicted, too, but did not realize it.

The next day, one of the sailors in my group, Vince, wanted to visit his aunt and uncle. They lived in a small town called Avalino. He asked me to join him and act as his interpreter. My Italian was not very good. I could more or less understand the language, but speaking was not my strength. Vince didn't speak a word of Italian, though, so I agreed to accompany him. I broke out the cigarettes again to bargain with the cab driver over the fare. I agreed to one pack to cover the fare but told him that he had to promise to take us back to Naples in the next two hours; then I'd give him another pack. In the house, Vince's relatives were trying to be hospitable by putting food in front of us. I told them I was not hungry, but Vince ate all of the food. I tried to translate for Vince's relatives the information Vince told me about his family living in America.

Eventually, the cab showed up as scheduled—those cigarettes were mighty powerful. I asked Vince why he ate all of their food. I purposely said I wasn't hungry because I knew that there was a food shortage. I guess I kept friends that were not very bright because it made me look like the intelligent one.

Back at the hotel, my group of barnstormers were waiting on me. I decided to go back to the ship that night and try to extend my leave for three or four more days. I wanted to see my family's doctor, Dr. Presti. He had a beautiful villa in Rome and had delivered my two brothers and me into this world. To my surprise, the lieutenant agreed to my leave request. He was one of the officers that I dropped off in New York City when I was driving the commander. Politics works anywhere. I took the 10:00 AM train the next morning and did not arrive in Rome until 7:30 that night. The train stopped in every town on the way up to those mountains, taking almost seven hours to go a little over fifty miles. Once in Rome, I hailed a cab and gave the address to the driver. When I arrived, I tried to pay in American money but the cab driver said no, he wanted Italian liras. (I think that he was the only man in all of Italy who would refuse U.S. money.) When Dr. Presti greeted me at the door, I had to ask him for liras to pay the driver.

Mrs. Presti made me a delicious dinner. There was obviously no shortage of food in his home. Following dinner, Dr. Presti took me on a tour of his beautiful villa with its large rooms. I noticed scrape marks on the tile floors, and he told me that the Germans had converted his villa into a headquarters during the war. He also told me that he had to buy all of his food on the black market, but that he could not get any cigarettes. I burst out laughing, as he looked at me, bewildered.

"Get my pea coat out of the closet," I said, and when he handed it to me, I pulled out two cartons of cigarettes and put them on the table. He tried to hand me three one-hundred-dollar bills. "Forget it!" I said, and he was stunned when I told him, "They cost me eighty cents. We only pay forty cents a carton out at sea."

In 1946, even doctors did not know much about lung cancer, which is why he smoked. In the morning, he took me to the Vatican to see Pope Pius XII. Dr. Presti belonged to a society that was granted an audience to see the pope. I was thrilled and enjoyed it very much. It was Easter Sunday.

Afterward, I took the train to return to Naples, but the return trip only took three hours—it was all downhill and not many stops. When I arrived, I met Morris Rabkin. He said the scuttlebutt was that the ship was going to stay in Naples another ten days. He asked me for a carton of cigarettes to get him through.

I responded, "Did you forget that I told you not to sell your cigarettes in Greece? You came back with that silly grin on your face after you sold them for three dollars a carton. Now suffer! I still have fifteen cartons in my locker aboard ship. I am going to sell most of them. What I have left, we will have plenty of fun with. After all, we spent over two years at sea without women and song. You can stay with me. It will not cost you anything. Not that you deserve it, but I am a nice guy!"

CHAPTER 3

AFTER DISCHARGE

In May 1946, I was finally discharged from the navy. We all had to have blood drawn before we were discharged. I became a little suspicious when I saw the medical people helping some of the fellows to sit on chairs. When my turn came, they drew quite a bit of blood very quickly. I immediately passed out and fell to the floor. This was the first and last time that I fainted. I awoke on a chair. This reminded me of when I was out at sea, and I decided to get circumcised. I asked the sailors who went before me about the procedure, and they just told me that I would find out. Well, thanks a lot for scaring me.

Today, girls and boys of eighteen tell their parents that they are going to get their own pad. In my day, if I told my parents I was getting my own pad, they would have known I was bluffing—I had no money. World War II changed all that. The economy changed, and there was money to be had. When I came out of the navy, I bought my first car, a Packard Clipper, for $2,200. It really felt good to see people have a little extra money to spend after ten long years of the Depression.

Just before getting out of the navy, my brother Vince called me to ask me to get some white shirts in the ship's stores. He told me that suit shirts were unavailable, even if one had money. Luckily, the navy store had eight shirts left in our size. I bought them all for $1.50 each. When I arrived home, Vince told me that he had to wait eighteen months for a Buick that he had ordered. Three months before my discharge, I had already put an order in for a Packard Clipper. While I was in the navy, I had saved eighteen hundred dollars. My dad still had his 1940 Packard. The car had 164,000 miles on it—it was our only car, so the three of us used the car around the clock. Two weeks after returning home, I received a phone call from the Packard agency. The car that I had ordered had just arrived. I asked the salesman for the asking price on the car, and he said twenty-two hundred dollars; I only had eighteen hundred, so I asked my parents to loan me the difference, and they agreed. When I went to pick up the car at the agency, it was still on the trailer.

"That car is not the same color green that I ordered," I told the salesman. "I do not want the car."

The salesman said, "You'll be back."

I went home with my friend, who had come along to drive my dad's car back. "I think you're making a mistake," he said. "Cars are very hard to get. In fact, I heard that some people are paying as much as one thousand dollars to get salespeople to put their names in front of others to buy a Cadillac." The price was twenty-five hundred dollars, and people would pay over the asking price.

When I told my brother that I refused my car, he said, "You're crazy! I offered the Buick people five hundred dollars to get ahead of the list, and they refused. We should get back to the dealer."

When we arrived, the car was off the trailer and was washed and waxed. The color was what I originally wanted. The salesman said, "I am sorry, but the next person on the order is getting the car."

I was sick to my stomach, but the salesman started to laugh. "Why are you laughing?" I asked.

"I'm just kidding. I knew you would be back," he said, "and that you would be a future customer."

I thanked him, finished signing the paperwork, and took the car home. My brother liked the idea of a new car because he would use it every opportunity he had.

One evening, a few days after I'd been discharged from the service, I went to New York City to meet someone, traveling in the Lincoln Tunnel from New Jersey. Before I entered the service, there had been an ordinance that all cars traveling in the city would use only their parking lights. This was to prevent the enemy from seeing lights if they were flying over the city. As I came out of the tunnel, a policeman stopped me and said he was going to give me a ticket for not using my headlights.

"I thought the ordinance was still in effect," I said.

"That's no excuse," he responded, "and besides, I have to make my quota. The fine is very small."

"I do not care if it is ten cents," I retorted. "I will come to court and challenge this summons!"

When I was in front of the judge, he said, "You came all the way from New Jersey to avoid paying a two-dollar ticket?"

"Your honor," I answered, "when the officer said he had to fill his quota, I really became angry. Today, I paid four dollars to park my car, and I also paid fifty cents to pass through the tunnel. Your honor, it's a matter of principle."

The judge said, "Not guilty!"

I was helping my dad full time with the produce business. My brother still wanted to take time off. After a few months, I decided that I really wanted to go to college on the GI Bill to study to be a lawyer, but my dad was ill with tuberculosis. He had to be committed to a sanatorium.

Later, my mother had a tooth extracted, but she kept complaining about pain in her gums. I took her back to the dentist, who did a biopsy. A few days later, we were notified that she had third-stage cancer. I took her to our primary doctor, who recommended we take her to New York Hospital, opposite from Sloan-Kettering Hospital. She had another biopsy taken, and the results were the same. The doctor consulted me about her condition. In those days, doctors did not tell the patients directly of the procedures they would need. The doctor told me that he would have to remove my mother's jawbone, and a month later, he would remove one of her ribs to replace her jawbone. He also told me, however, that there was only one such case, to his knowledge, in which the operation had been successful. My job was to present my mother with this information.

When I told my mother what was to be done, she took it surprising well. She was sure brave. The operation went well, and she was hospitalized for three months. Her mouth was slightly disfigured afterward, but she lived thirty years longer and challenged the rages of cancer.

This was the end of my going to college to become a lawyer. I had to support my parents. It was very difficult for me to accept not going to college. I was a World War II veteran and could have gone to college free of charge. But for me, it was back to the grind. My dad had been infected for quite a few years with tuberculosis. He was in and out of sanatoriums for years. My mother would take all kinds of precautions when Dad stayed at home. She would have separate dishes, utensils glasses, towels, and so on. She did not want the family to get infected with TB. In the 1960s, when he was at the sanatorium, a new vaccine called stiptomycin came out. That helped him and other patients to cope with the disease. He was released from the sanatorium and came home where he lived to 1970.

He was seventy years old when he passed on. He probably would have lived longer if he had given up smoking. He lasted longer than his three younger brothers who died back in the 1940s and 50s from TB. Even when I was younger, I was aware that my father's brothers had died before they were thirty-five years old. That is why I invest in the biotech industry—to help scientists find vaccines. My son and I have invested our money into such companies because, not being a scientist, I want to help in other ways.

Our neighborhood had a social and athletic club. Our softball team was great, and we also had a talented football team. We were the talk of the city and were undefeated for several years. I participated in the softball games, but I was too small and too light for football. When it came to social affairs, I was right there on top. In January 1947, we ran our first dance. We rented the Newark Armory and hired Tony Pastor, the Eddy Gee bands, the Clooney sisters (including Rosemary), and Jack Leonard, who was formerly with Tommy Dorsey. We were able to get these entertainers through the Morris Agency in New York City. They gave us a reasonable price because it was right after New Year's. We had thirty days to promote this affair. The name of the club was the Revelers Social and Athletic Club. We advertised in every town surrounding Newark, New Jersey. We placed hundreds of placards in buses and stores. Our biggest concern was whether we could sell enough tickets to pay for the event. None of us had any experience with this new type of venture. We held a meeting to decide on the charge for each ticket. I was the treasurer and estimated that the price should be at least two dollars per person. The board voted it down and decided on $1.60 per ticket.

The night of the dance finally arrived, and we all had worried looks on our faces. That afternoon, the weather report was very disheartening—rain or snow was predicted for the evening. Instead, it became an ice storm that started at about 5:00 PM. Every member on the committee, including me, arrived at the armory early. Doors opened at 7:00 PM, and believe it or not, when we looked outside there were thousands of people waiting to get in, standing in line in that ice storm. We had to tell the security person in charge to get more help or police in order to control the crowd. At 8:30 PM, people were still filing in, even with the hazardous roads and cold, icy weather. We had a turnout of over ten thousand people. They came from all over, even as far as Philadelphia. The only mishap that entire night was when the clothing racks caved in, and three women lost their fur coats in the melee. We reimbursed them a total of twelve hundred dollars. Fur coats back then were not as expensive as nowadays. Even so, we still made a profit of four thousand dollars. For the next three years, we ran dances that were successful, although they did not draw as large a crowd as that first dance.

Ninety-eight percent of our members were veterans of WW II, and after a couple of years, they were starting to settle down. Every other week, it seemed that one of the members would get married. Little by little, the membership diminished. I was the last president, and in 1951, I decided that it was time for the club to disband. The club had a pretty good thirteen-year run. And then, just as love found Andy Hardy, love was about to find me.

CHAPTER 4

LOVE AND FAMILY LIFE

I started dating a couple of girls. Rosalyn was a real beauty, with natural black hair, green eyes, and a light complexion. All the fellows would drool whenever she passed the corner where we would hang out. She did not realize her beauty. None of us had the nerve to approach her. I happened to hear from one of the boys that she was interested in music. A few days later, I saw her waiting for a bus, and I pulled my car over to the curb. I got out of the car, walked straight over to her, and asked her if I could give her a ride. She said she wanted to go to Stanton's Nightclub in Newark. She'd heard that Bob Eberle, formerly with the Jimmy Dorsey's band, was performing there. Luckily, I knew Bob Eberle because I had hired him for a couple of the club dances. When I told her that I knew Bob Eberle and would give her a ride, she flipped. I knew that from then on, I was in with her.

We arrived at Stanton's Nightclub just as Bob started a set. We were sitting at the bar, and I excused myself to go to the men's room. On the way, Bob, who had finished his last number, came up to shake my hand. I took the opportunity to ask Bob to give me a little buildup with Rosalyn. I went to the men's room and stalled for a while so Bob would have some time to talk to Rosalyn. When I walked back to the bar, I passed Bob, and he told me that I was all set. Rosalyn was at the bar and looked like she was on cloud nine. She asked me why I hadn't told her that I was responsible for getting Bob Eberle and Helen O'Connell their singing jobs with the Jimmy Dorsey band. She said that she had no idea that I had so many connections in the music world. I sat there and listened to her, knowing that the only connection I had was the Morris Agency in New York. I hired bands through them; otherwise, I had absolutely no connections in the music field. Rather than lie, I told her that I did not want to talk about music at that time. Even so, she was so impressed by whatever Bob had said that she stuck to me like glue.

After that night, we dated for about six months. When we toured different nightclubs, her beauty drew attention. I was not a handsome dude but not bad looking either. My only drawback was my height, but I compensated with my outgoing personality. My friends would ask me how I could keep her with all the competition around. They never knew—she didn't want to get into the music business; she just wanted to be with someone who had any affiliation with it. Thanks to Bob Eberle, I was the one to fit the bill.

Other than Rosalyn, it was very easy to get dates with girls because I had a reputation as a great lover. I hope I did not disappoint anyone. I dated another girl named Vilma, off and on, for several years. I was not ready to get married, although her mother was pressuring her to get me to marry her. I cared for her, but I was not in a position to marry at that time. My parents were both ill, and my finances were not good. She became tired of waiting, but we remained friends. One day, she told me she was going to get married. In fact, she invited me to her wedding. I wished her luck and accepted the invitation.

I remember when my friends and I were single, we did not have much money to go out on dates with girls, but drinks were very economical—rum and Coke was twenty-five cents. One time, I was on a double date—my date, and a friend of mine and his date. I ordered four drinks, and my friend excused himself. Fifteen minutes passed and he still had not returned. I left the table to look for him—and found him eating a hot dog. I told him, "You left us stranded!"

He said, "I wasn't going to treat them to food."

"Get that cheap habit out of your system," I told him. But all his life, it never left him.

The girls I dated as a teenager would mostly drink soda pop. Once in a while, a date wanted to be daring and have a stronger drink. After I had been gone for three years in the navy during the war, I came back to a much different lifestyle. Girls were driving cars and drinking hard liquor. They were older by then, though, so I guess it was okay.

A year went by, and my brothers and I still were struggling with the family business. My brother wanted to expand, which we did. Unfortunately, we tried to do so too fast, which put us almost in bankruptcy. Luckily, I was successful in establishing new chain-store customers, which enabled us to get back on our feet.

During this time, it seemed like all my friends were getting married. I was best man at several weddings. One night, I was at the Elks Club dance and ran into one of the girls I had known for quite some time. "When are you planning on getting married?" she asked me. "Most of your friends already are married."

"My mother had me until I was eighteen years old," I told her, "and the navy had me until I was twenty-one years old. Now, I need some breathing room. I'm concentrating on improving the family business and have plenty of time to get married later."

Adele, a friend who I would see at the dances, introduced me to Marge, who was Adele's cousin. I guess it was love at first sight. She was beautiful. So I *was* a goner, right at the start. Marge had beautiful blue eyes and pretty blonde hair. How could I resist? On our first date, I took her to see Sammy Davis Jr. at a local nightclub. We got along great, right from the first date, and we dated for about a year. While we were dating, my older brother, Vince, got married. Naturally, Marge started to put the pressure on me to get married, too. I was running out of excuses, so I gave in. We were married on Valentine's Day in 1953. One year later, in March 1954, my first son, Joseph, was born. My second son, Tony, was born in August 1956.

As of this writing, Marge and I have been happily married for fifty-six years. Years ago, some women would stay married because they needed their husbands to support them and their families. If a married women worked, she was frowned at because her place was in the home. That just the way it was in those days. My wife, Marge, however, is a wonderful wife and mother. She is beautiful and understanding and has done a great job raising our two sons. That is why we are still in love after fifty-six years of marriage.

People ask, "What is the secret to stay married that long?" All I can say is that we have a give-and-take marriage. We show respect to one another.

During our marriage we've had some sad times, though. A tragedy happened when Marge's nephew Freddy was shot and killed in 1967, when there were race riots in Newark, New Jersey. He was a detective. His wife called our home, saying he'd hurt his leg in an incident. The next morning as I was heading to work, I saw National Guard units walking on Market Street with rifles, and some shooting was going on. When I arrived at my place of business, I immediately called Freddy's house and told his wife not to let him leave the house.

She said, "You know him—duty comes first."

A few hours later, we got the news that he and a fireman had been killed. Freddy was only thirty-one years old. He left a wife and two children. He was a great guy; he would do anyone a favor. He was my wife's favorite nephew. That was a sad time in our lives, as was the tragedy that occurred a few months later. My wife's sister Helen fell asleep while smoking in bed. Ninety percent of her body was burned. Helen passed away in the hospital a few days later. She had a German shepherd that had jumped though the second-floor glass window to escape the fire. He was lucky and survived his escape.

On June 15, 2009, my wife's niece, who was being treated for kidney failure and was on dialysis, passed away. Her treatment had not been successful—her body was receiving unwanted fluids, and she suffered tremendous pain. She decided to discontinue dialysis treatment. Her doctor's approval of her decision convinced her to get ready for death. She was brave and said, "I am at peace now." She passed away three days later.

My wife was very upset over her passing, especially over her telling my wife she was ready to die

In 1955, I took a business trip to Cuba, looking for products to import to the United States. The products I found were not of the quality we needed, so I had to pass. Then, I made a trip to Guatemala and found unbelievable conditions. I met an American pilot who had used his plane to help the president of Guatemala to intimidate the opposition. His reward was one hundred acres of hemp land, which he had continued to grow. I met him in the

Panama Hotel. He tried to convince me to stay and run some of his enterprises. He flew me in his plane to the west coast of the country, where he owned many shrimp boats, in addition to a processing plant to freeze the shrimp. He wanted me to run the shrimp operation. He offered to make me a full partner and said that I wouldn't need to invest any money in the company. Every two weeks, a ship would come to port to pick up all the shrimp that had been processed. He showed me the contracts he had with a company in San Francisco, and it looked very profitable.

"Why do you think I deserve the honor of running your business?" I asked.

"Guatemalan natives were not capable of running a business," he explained. "I need a businessperson."

"I am interested," I told him, "but I have a wife and child in Miami. This is a decision that I will have to consider very seriously."

He then took me to a nice home and said that I could have the house. It came equipped with two maids, a butler, and a gardener. The overhead cost was next to zero. I could not believe that the workers were paid forty cents a day for a full day's work of shrimping. (This may be why the country went through a revolution every ten years.) Guatemala also had an abundance of mahogany trees, which was a very lucrative export product. The pilot told me that if I would stay there, running his operation for five to seven years, I could become a multimillionaire. He was already very wealthy, which convinced me that he was telling the truth. Still, it was a difficult decision.

I was very excited about the situation when I returned to Miami, where Marge and fifteen-month-old Joseph were waiting for me. I told Marge about the situation, but she was not interested. Later, I spoke with my congressman about the situation in Guatemala, and he told me that the U.S. government would advance me $200,000 to set up a company and employ the local people in Guatemala. There were hundreds of people out of work in that country. The rationale was that if the Guatemalan natives were employed, then it would keep them from turning to Communism. The Cold War was on, and the United States was trying to keep the Russian influence out of Central America. I saw an opportunity to start a company that exported mahogany to the United States.

Still, Marge would not agree to it. Her excuse was that her mother was elderly, and she did not want to leave her behind. She also did not want our son to grow up in Guatemala. She was pregnant, so I had no other choice but to agree. To this day, I still think about what would have happened if we had gone. One thing is for sure; I would speak Spanish fluently.

My second son, Anthony, was born in 1956. It was a nice feeling to see the boys grow up. I was the coach of my sons' Little League teams. Every time they would win a game, I would take them to the local Dairy Queen and treat them to an ice cream. One evening, we played an extra-inning game, and I was running a little late. I brought the boys and some of their teammates to our usual Dairy Queen. The sun had already set, so it was nearly dark. One mother was waiting in front of her house when I dropped her boy off. She told me that I had some nerve, bringing her son home so late. It took all I had to keep my anger at bay when I said to her, "Ma'am, if you or your husband would show some interest in your son and come to the games, then he would get home earlier. Is this the thanks I get for babysitting your son?"

Actually, most of the parents didn't show up for the games because they were too busy with their own social lives. Then they wondered why their kids would later get into trouble with drugs. I guess I am from the old school. I believe in spending time with my children.

We were very fortunate with our sons—they both turned out to be great guys. My older son, Joe, always excelled in school. He graduated from MIT with two degrees, then went on to Harvard School of Medicine, where he received his medical degree. Later, he completed his residency and practiced medicine for a short time before going into research. My wife was disappointed by this decision. She had wanted him to become a surgeon, but I told her that he would only be successful in work that interested him. Joe relocated to Cold Spring Harbor Labs in Long Island, New York, and for about a year, he worked with Dr. Watson, one of the scientists who discovered DNA.

Joe seemed to be getting quite a few colds because the wintertime in Cold Spring Harbor was very damp and cold. He wrote an article that was published in the *New England Journal of Medicine*, which was noticed by a scientist in La Jolla, California, who was affiliated with the Scripps Research Institute. The scientist came to Cold Spring Harbor to recruit Joe and offered him a three-year contract and an increase in pay. Joe asked me what he should do, and I advised him to move to California, partly because of the warm weather—which would be better for his health—and partly because the increase in pay he was offered was two and half times more than what he was currently receiving. He took my advice and went to California. He was assigned to Scripps Lab and supervised about twenty other scientists. He seemed quite content with the move he had made.

Tony graduated from University of Pennsylvania, and had some studies at the Wharton School of Business. After college, he received business experience with my import company. He tried that for a few years but although he was making money, he seemed restless. One day, he told Marge and me that he was going to California to join Joe. We did not object. Marge told him to find some kind of business and settle in California.

Tony later reported back to me about some of the businesses he was investigating. The first one had great potential; it was in the cell phone industry. This, however, was back in the 1980s, and there were all kinds of government regulations and red tape involved. The business would have taken years to develop. Tony also investigated other possibilities, but nothing materialized. He still wanted to do something in the business world. To Tony's credit, he encouraged Joe to try the biotech business. He and Joe considered starting a biotech company in San Diego. Joe's contract was about to expire with Scripps, which would allow him the freedom to pursue his and Tony's business plan. They approached me about their idea; I told them they should take the chance.

Looking around me these days, sometimes I think I fell asleep for sixty years. Everything has changed. My wife and I feel we do not belong here anymore. I remember when Hollywood had to get permission from the Hays Office (which set of industry censorship guidelines) for Clark Gable to say, "Frankly, my dear, I don't give a damn" in Gone With the Wind. How things have changed. My wife and I are not squares; we are hip to everything. We just do not like where the population is going. Twenty-four years ago when I settled in California, I went into restaurants wearing a jacket and tie; even then, people looked at me as if I was from another planet. Maybe the trend will change again someday, and people will dress again like my wife and I do, wearing dresses and jackets.

Today, Marge and I have six grandchildren—four boys and two girls: Tina (age 22, as of this writing), Lauren (15), Andy (21), Anthony (17), Danny (16), and Matthew (11). We enjoy them immensely. Watching them grow up and watching their participation in sports—baseball, football, soccer, basketball—is a real pleasure. They keep us pretty busy, trying to keep up with their schedules. They ask me, "Pop-Pop, are you coming to watch me play?" I enjoy watching them play and try to attend as many games I can. I hope that Marge and I live long enough to see all our grandchildren graduate college. So far, Tina graduated on May 1, 2009. That is the reward and enjoyment in having grandchildren.

I enjoy spoiling my grandchildren; I do not want them to wish for material things the way I did when I was their age. The other day, my fifteen-year-old granddaughter asked me to give her ten dollars. I asked, "What do you need the money for?"

She said, "I do not want the money now. My parents give me an allowance. I want to earn the money on my own. Can I wash your car this Saturday for ten dollars?"

I agreed. My grandson, who is eleven years old, heard the conversation and asked, "Can I wash Grandma's car for five dollars?" Competition is great!

It's said that when we get old, we are in our "golden years." Even with all the aches and pains that come with aging, having your grandchildren love you makes it worth it all. I am very thankful that I am healthy enough to enjoy the children.

Matt one day asked, "Will you take me to Toys-R-Us?" He had a toy in mind that he saw on television. Approaching the entrance of the store I said, "Remember, only one toy." There was no response from him. After looking in the store, he got the toy he wanted. Then he spotted another toy and, looking at me with his innocent eyes, he asked, "Can I have this also?" Naturally, I succumbed to his wishes. On leaving the store, I said, "Matt, I thought we agreed to only one toy." He responded, "I did not agree." Leave it to the cunning of the young.

All in all, I enjoy every minute of the experience I have with my grandchildren. I just hope that the younger generations will have a better world when we are gone. Every person should strive for a better world. We veterans in all the wars did our best to defend America's freedom and to make a better world for our children and grandchildren.

CHAPTER 5

THE BIOTECH BUSINESS AND LIFE IN CALIFORNIA TODAY

I have been in California for twenty-four years. As of this writing, I am eighty-four-years old now and still going strong. My business background was in importing produce (fruits)—that is the most competitive business that I know. I was in that business for more than forty years. There was a saying, "Move the merchandise, or it will move you." All products were perishable. The pressure was continuously on my mind.

When I was sixty years old, I left New Jersey and came to California to join in a venture with my sons, Joseph and Tony. They were starting a biotech company. I have to give Tony credit as the one with the initial idea to start the company. They asked Marge and me to come to San Diego to help them out. When we arrived in California, our sons were in the process of looking for a place to set up their small lab. I invested some money to help them get started and then returned to the East Coast, but I kept in touch with them to see how things were progressing. They found a small place to rent and set up shop. Most important, they came up with a product that the scientific community all over the world wanted to buy.

I joined them as a founder of the company. I was the treasurer, buyer, and point person for the company. I did not have a college education, but that did not hinder me. I had plenty of experience in business, which I applied to purchasing materials from other vendors—they were surprised when I would bargain with them, but that is all I did for forty years in my business.

I had to give up the business I was in with my brothers, and Vince was not happy with my choice to leave. I sold my portion of the business for quite a bit less than my share was worth. Now, here I was, sixty years old and taking a chance on a new venture, not knowing what was in store for me.

After a couple years of organizing the business, my sons and I became successful. The company grew at an unbelievable pace. After five years, we expanded the workspace from 800 square feet to 50,000 square feet, in addition to opening branches in England and Germany. Our sales multiplied daily. I often thought about how much my family had to struggle in the 1950s. A business back then grew at a much slower pace. The growth rate of the business I had with my sons, however, was astounding. They accomplished an incredible amount in such a short period. I am very proud of both of them. The company made products for scientists all around the world. We were also involved in the research of several diseases. The company received several honors and recognition by the local

biotech community.

As I've mentioned, I was the buyer for our biotech company. I was familiar with a vendor that sold a product at a cost of fifty-eight hundred dollars. One day, I found a purchase order for this product from one of our scientists at a cost of sixty-eight hundred dollars—he had called it in without my knowledge. I knew we had been overcharged, but the scientist did not know what I knew about this vendor—he was a wheeler-dealer like me.

I called the scientist into my office and said, "You are getting into a field you that you are not familiar with. You were overcharged for that product." He couldn't believe it and challenged me, wanting to bet our paychecks, mine against his, that he was right.

I made a call to the vendor and told him to cancel that order. When he asked why I was canceling, I told him that he had overcharged my employee. I had my speakerphone on so my employee could hear the conversation, and I told the vendor, "You know that I have been the only one purchasing this product. We have been paying fifty-eight hundred dollars for it."

The vendor said "The price went up."

I knew this was a lie, and I told him that I had another company that was willing to sell me the same product for fifty-two hundred dollars—that was also a lie.

"Hold on," the vendor said. A couple of minutes later, he came back to our conversation, saying, "You can have the product for five thousand. I've obtained it cheaper from my supplier."

I agreed, and that was the end of the transaction—but my employee, who had bet me his paycheck, was now turning red, thinking I was going to take his paycheck.

I said to him, "Many years ago, the Greyhound Bus Company had a commercial with the catch phrase, 'Leave the driving to us.' I do not come into the lab and tell you how to make experiments. Leave the purchasing to me."

I think he learned his lesson.

In 1947, I was in Haiti, staying in a very modest hotel. There, I met a man from the United Nations. He was taking a survey of the conditions in Haiti. I was shocked when he told me the reports he was recording for the UN—that the average life span for a male was twenty-six years old; that the sanitation was horrible— their human waste was in ditches in front of their tin-roof huts. Disease ran rampant in all parts of the country. Their leader had a beautiful mansion on ten acres of land, guarded by a fence and army soldiers, who were well paid. The politicians and the soldiers ran the government. The government was corrupt, top to bottom. Children were only allowed third-grade educations, and they were taught that when they grew up, they were to work and pay taxes. The government kept the population ignorant all the time. When the government found out that the UN person was making reports about conditions in Haiti, he was told to leave ... or else.

I was there for different reasons. Some Americans that lived there told me to keep my mouth shut, or I would not leave the island alive. My only interest at the time was to get products for our import company. The Americans told me that if I wanted to do business in Haiti, I would have to pay the politicians. Nothing left the island unless a politician was paid in advance. So, I went to speak to a politician—I still remember his name: Tippenhaur.

He said, "Before you speak to any of the farmers, you have to give me ten thousand dollars."

I said, "If I do, what guarantee do I have that I will get the merchandise?"

He said, "None."

The farmers probably had to pay him, too. I declined the deal because I did not feel comfortable in that kind of business climate.

Later on, in New York, I did business with a shrewd businessman named Sol Pollitz. I told him about my business experience in Haiti, and he started to laugh.

I asked, "What are you laughing about?"

He said, "It is not funny, but I lost twenty-five thousand dollars to those crooks a year ago. I gave Tippenhaur the money. I chartered a refrigerated ship to pick up the mangos and bananas, but when the ship arrived, there was no product."

Sol went to Tippenhaur and wanted his money back. He was refused. He lost the money he'd paid Tippenhaur, as well as the cost to charter the ship. He later went to the State Department to complain. Their answer was, "Do you want us to start a war over your business deal?" Sol was a successful businessman; he did all right. And he learned his lesson. I just escaped a bad deal, but I don't doubt that others were taken in on such schemes.

When my wife and I first came to California, we were lonely. We would send plane tickets to our friends back East so they could come and stay with us for a while. The people here in California are laid back, but we didn't find them to be very friendly. I still cannot figure out why some of them act so strange. I have socialized with several on different occasions with same results. We go to dinner with them and pick up the check, but they don't seem to want to go out again. Marge and I always do our best to make others feel comfortable, but many of the people we've met seem to act as if they're hiding something from their past. It also took us several months to find a decent restaurant that served quality food. That has changed in the last few years, but it's still not on the same level as back East.

My parents bought their first house in 1944 for $8700. In 1960, I purchased my first house for $21,000. Then in 1963, I purchased a house for $31,500. It was half brick and half wood.

It had a swimming pool and was landscaped beautifully. It was in a nice neighborhood—we raised our two sons there. I sold that house in 1977 for $85,000, then purchased a condo for $150,000. Eight years later, I sold the condo for $300,000. Then, in 1985, I moved to California to be with my sons. I rented for about five years, but finally saw a house in a nice neighborhood, selling for $450,000. I thought the price was too high. Less than two years later, I purchased that same house for $675,000. I can only imagine what I might get for the sale of that house today in this inflated market. I feel sorry for young married couples that purchase homes at high prices. These houses are built today are often constructed with inferior materials. They are not worth $200,000, yet the public buys every house they build.

About ten years ago, I received a call from a friend of mine named Roberto. He owned a restaurant where I would go for lunch. He invited me to his place, saying, "Mohammed Ali is waiting for you in a booth to have lunch."

I said, "Roberto, you are putting me on."

He said, "No, I'm not. Would I lie to you?"

Well, curiosity made me go. Lo and behold, Ali was sitting in the booth and waved me over to sit with him. I knew Roberto had set this up. So, Ali and I had lunch together.

He said to me, "See that table over there?" There were about ten men talking. "My manager is sitting with them. He thinks I am going to sign up to make commercials. They are wasting their time, because I am not going to make any commercials. I do not need the money."

After we had lunch, he handed me a collection of papers to read. He was trying to convert me to the religion of Islam. I told him I would read the papers, but I would not promise to convert. He was very cordial and spoke in a slow, low tone. He was suffering from Parkinson's disease. One of the patrons had a camera and photographed Ali and me. I had many copies made of that photo and sent them to all my friends back East. I still keep a photo in my office.

Did you ever go into a deal with a partner who was reluctant to take risks? One day, a partner and I decided to purchase a race horse. We went to the yearly auction. My partner said, "Twenty thousand dollars is our limit. Ten thousand each."

I did not answer him. When bidding time came, he became excited over a horse and told our trainer to start bidding. I told them to wait for next horse coming up. They disagreed. So, reluctantly I went along with the bid. We were able to get the horse for $19,500. That may my partner very happy.

The reason I was not excited was because the name of the next horse impressed me. His name was No Nukes. He went for $22,000; only $2,500 more than the horse we purchased. I kept telling my partner, "We should have bought No Nukes."

He said, "We bought our horse cheaper."

Unfortunately for us, No Nukes went on to make five million dollars in less than two years. He was a champion. Also, after he was retired, he made millions in breeding. To have a horse bred by him cost $100,000. Every time my partner saw me, he would put his head down, but it was partly my fault for not insisting that we bid on No Nukes. The horse we did purchase made enough for his keep, but I learned my lesson: when I have a hunch, I should keep to it.

I always wonder about gamblers and the way they think. A friend and I would go to a small race track in Freehold, New Jersey. He was a World War II veteran, too, and had serious back pains. He was a pharmacist with a prosperous business.

When we went to the track, I would leave my car with the valet—in those days, it only cost two dollars plus a one-dollar tip. One day, I went alone and gave my car to the valet. I happened to turn around, and I saw my friend walking from the public parking, which was at least two thousand yards away from the track entrance. When he arrived, after a slow, painful walk, I asked him, "Why didn't you use the valet?"

He said, "Why should I give them two dollars?"

I was in total shock; I knew he could afford it easily. I invited him to sit at my table, but he declined. After a few races, I descended to the public betting area, where I saw him at the betting window. He bet fifty dollars on a horse that lost. I tapped him on the shoulder and told him to come with me to the club lounge—for a seven- or eight-dollar charge, I could have all the comforts, and the staff addressed me as Mr. Sorge when I enter the lounge.

My friend said he would not give them five dollars just to sit at a table and have lunch. He was not cheap—he could lose hundreds of dollars by gambling and think very little about it.

When I moved to California, I encountered another gambler who had me thinking that gamblers are stupid. I was playing poker in an Indian casino, and one hand was getting hot and heavy. I had a poor hand, so I dropped out. This one fellow was raising the pot for big money, and another was challenging him. Between the two of them, they probably put in over two hundred dollars each. As they were playing, a waitress arrived with food that one of them had ordered. When the man who ordered the food saw the bill, he went into a rage and told the waitress that yesterday, the same meal had cost $1.75 less. She responded that the food had been on special yesterday.

I could not hold back; I told this guy off. I said, "You put in over two hundred dollars in the pot, and you have the nerve to upset that poor girl for $1.75? Do not tell me to mind my own business. I just had to shame you."

He felt embarrassed and did not confront me.

These gamblers are a strange lot. When it comes to spending money other than gambling, they are very frugal. I guess they have to be frugal, just to keep their gambling habit going. One of my friends back East told me a story about another gambler. His wife passed away, and he sold his house for $350,000—it was a very nice house. In less than two months, however, he lost all his money by gambling on horses. He was known by the name Mike TV. He would repair TVs. He would bring customers' TVs to his shop to repair; then, he would tell the customer that it would be too expensive to repair and that he would trash the TV. In reality, he would fix the TV and sell it—he did this to get money for gambling, and he was able to get away with that for some time, until one day, a customer came to his shop and beat him to a pulp. He was hospitalized for ten days..

I have been gambling for sixty years. on and off, yet I will never become a degenerate. I gamble for recreation and can take it or leave it. I guess gambling is a sickness for some people, like any other disease. Most of them are infected with the thought that they will become wealthy someday. All I know is that 98 percent of people who are successful in their lives achieved it from straight, honest, hard work. The other 2 percent either inherited money or stole or defrauded it from someone and are probably serving time in jail.

When I moved to California in 1985, I kept in touch with quite a few members of our old social club. All I would hear from them was "When I am sixty-five, I will retire." I would tell them not to retire; that they had to keep their brains exercised, not just their bodies. I would tell them, "You are going to sit home, watch television, and become a vegetable." Today, out of one hundred members, there are only six of us still living.

I had a cousin we called Red because he had red hair. He always made funny remarks. Unfortunately, he had heart problems. When I visited him in the hospital, he told me that a Catholic priest had been in to see him. The priest wanted Red to confess his sins. Red told the priest, "Put me down for a little of everything." He always had a pleasant attitude. He passed away a few days later. That was quite a few years ago, but I still miss him.

I am a firm believer that a person should work if he or she is able. Today, I work five days a week, even at the age of eighty-four. My wife asks me when I am going to retire. I tell her I will retire when they throw the dirt over me.

CHAPTER 6

SOME THOUGHTS ABOUT WHAT I'VE LEARNED FROM LIFE

Today, the younger generation has no idea what their grandparents went through and the sacrifices they made. When they hear stories from their grandparents' day, they might frown and say, "There they go again, trying to convince us how hard they had it during the Depression."

ON DISCRIMINATION AND RACISM

I was discriminated against when I was young boy because my grandparents came from Italy. I was called a Wop and a Dago. Right up to today, I get cracks like, "Are you in the Mafia?" In my discussions with black employees, I would tell them to just ignore people who called them racial slurs. Such people are ignorant. Can I help it if some Italian immigrants were held down many years and decided to start the so-called Mafia? They preyed on their own people at their beginnings in New York City. My grandfather was almost a victim of their threatening tactics. Somehow, he was not bothered anymore because someone who was not in the Mafia did a favor for one of those gangs. My grandfather was in business, and they wanted to extort him for money weekly. Remember, that was in the early 1920s. There is such a small percentage of people in the so-called Mafia today, yet they leave a stigma on all Americans of Italian descent.

I look back at what my grandparents on my dad's side had to endure: no education, no money, unable to speak the language, no welfare. They struggled and worked it out. They did not know what discrimination meant. Most Italians brought to this country things like music and art and trades, like masonry, carpentry, etc. They were greeted with discriminatory slurs. I do not remember any Italian immigrants complaining about America. They were happy to be in this country. Most of them made sure that their children received an education. The fortunate ones, who were able to go to college, were discriminated against because they were of Italian descent. Some students today get free tuition and free lodging. Still, there is continual whining. They need a depression to educate them.

Other nationalities are just as guilty of having mafias. Judges, politicians, and police take bribes to protect the gangs of every race. All I can say to black Americans is stop whining, get off your butts, get an education, and become someone. There are no excuses today. Colleges make it easy for blacks to get admitted. I remember fifty years ago, my uncle was refused admittance to quite a few colleges because of his Italian parents. He tried and tried and finally was admitted to a college (they probably needed the money). He kept on going to school and became a lawyer. So stop feeling sorry for yourself. You can make it. There are so many opportunities today to get ahead. There are no excuses.

Look at sports today. Blacks and others make millions in basketball, football, and baseball. Oprah, rap artists, and many others are making plenty of money. So don't make the excuse that because you are black, brown ,yellow, or any other color that you are being held down. Fifty years ago I would have agreed but not in this day and age.

Time sure does fly by. When I reminisce about when I was young and going to the movies to watch cowboy pictures, Hollywood was either racist or using psychological colors on the cowboys' dress to make us believe who were the bad guys—the bad guys were always dressed in black or dark colors, wore black hats, and rode black or dark horses. The heroes always had light clothes and white hats and rode white horses. That came as close to portraying that the minorities were bad as anything. Hollywood was guilty of discrimination, especially with the blacks being portrayed as ignorant. That was during 1930s and 1940s. Then, later on, they made movies in which the whites always were prejudiced against the blacks. There were certainly cases of that in the South. I grew up in the North and never saw any blacks being mistreated by whites. In fact, in our import business, in which I spent forty years, we employed over seventy-five people who were ethnic minorities. If any are still living today, they would say they were treated with respect and humility. Today, Hollywood goes to great lengths to show minorities how bad a few individuals were treating them fifty years ago. Maybe Hollywood is trying to make up for the racism in films that they made many years ago.

Today, we hear about how the Native Americans were in America first. What difference does it make who was here first or last? We are here now. So everybody should get along. Many so-called civil rights activists keep fueling the hatred. There are good and bad people in every race.

Some slick leaders use every opportunity to exploit every situation. Let us start with the African Americans. I do not know why they use that term: African. I never met one black who came from Africa. I spent forty years in the ghetto in our importing business. We employed 90 percent blacks and 10 percent whites. Our business was unionized, so critics cannot say we hired blacks because we paid them less than whites. The employees received all the same wages.

Many races have been discriminated over the years including many minorities discriminating against white people. Take Hurricane Katrina in New Orleans, for example. White people in helicopters were risking their lives to save black people. Whites donated millions of dollars to help hurricane victims, white or black. There are always activists inflaming the people with their lies. These are the people who want to keep the poor and ignorant down. Promise them more government goodies, so they will vote for a particular party. Democrats do not want the poor to become educated, because they would see for themselves what is really going on. On the other hand, the educated minorities are getting wise to these falsehoods. They are living better lives, because they are helping themselves. I know about discrimination firsthand. When I was aboard ship in the navy, black sailors could not hold any rank. Their job was to serve the officers—for example, serve their meals. There were 225 officers on the ship, and not one was an Italian American. There was one Jewish officer. I do not know how he was able to get in. Politics, I assume. The black sailors were treated all right, but they had to risk their lives, just like the rest of us, when the Japanese suicide planes hit us. Finally, in 1946, that all started to change when discrimination was banned in the armed services. All I have to say now is that minorities should get that hate against the white folks out of their systems. This generation had nothing to do with treatment of minorities down South. Stop your whining and get with it. You should have lived in the Depression of the1930s. People did not have to discriminate. They were struggling to pay the rent and feed their families. They could not sit on their butts and whine to the government for handouts. You hear stories that children supposedly are starving today. Tell me: where are they starving in this country? They get food stamps, so no children should starve. When I go into supermarkets, I see shoppers with baskets that are filled to the top. This is more propaganda against the government. I have been around a long time, and I see the abuses people get away with and still complain. They should live in some Third World country where the rule is "no work, no food." Today, that is not politically appropriate to mention. It is the truth. The so-called poor are spoiled.

Today, the Arabs in this country are happy because they were oppressed in their homeland, but here in the good old USA, they make a good living and get things out of life for themselves and their children. In their homeland, they are taught to hate anyone who does not believe in their religion. I know a few Middle Easterners; they think Americans are stupid for complaining. We are free to practice our religion, go into business, etc. People do not realize how great it is to have freedom. We only realize it when we lose it. There are many so-called leaders in this world who use religion to manipulate their populations to hate each other: the Arabs against the Jews; the Jews against WASPs and vice versa, the KKK against Catholics and blacks; blacks against whites. It's all stupidity. We are all going to die someday, so why hate each other?

On Illegal Aliens and Terrorists

Things were so different when I was a young boy. I guess the country was looking for people to come to the United States. We had plenty of room for them. Now, it's fifty thousand soldiers to our southern border, and twenty thousand to the Canadian border. This step is not only to keep the Latinos out but the terrorists who constantly sneak in our country and form headquarters here. It might take them a few years, but they will try to kill us on a large scale. If we really want to stem the tide, just announce there will be no more goodies, like welfare, free medical care, education, etc. The illegals that are here that have jobs do not need welfare. They are happy, and do not want to disrupt anything.

About two months ago, I wrote a letter to my local congressman who was running for president. In this letter, I told him what to say when he was on television in the first debate in Iowa. He was always talking about building a thirty-foot fence along the border with Mexico. I told him the illegals would build a thirty-two-foot ladder. They have no fear of being apprehended. Our pinheads in DC have no desire to build a fence.

All I know is that people from all over the world are trying to get into the United States. I hear every day about illegals crossing the borders with no problems. We are inviting terrorists to come in and destroy us. I have heard that England, France, and Italy are deporting hate-mongers and terrorists. Meanwhile, our politicians—Democrats and Republicans—are sitting on their hands because they all want the Latino vote. If the terrorists get enough strength to really cripple our country and force our economy into a crisis, the Latino vote will not mean a hill of beans. Our politicians better wake up and start doing something soon; otherwise, the American public will start doing something to correct this problem. They want to protect their families and their way of life. Life is precious to people in America. In some countries, life is cheap.

Some people say we cannot bring change to the Middle East. They have been that way for thousands of years. I have to differ with them, because the Japanese, after World War II, were changed from their old customs. For example, before the war, women had to walk in public behind men. Today, that is longer valid. They dress like the Western world. Things can change all the time.

Today, illegals are demanding their rights, but they have no rights. They come into the United States, receive welfare, free medical care, and free education. Some are hard-working people, but they should apply legally to live here. These illegals should demonstrate in Mexico, where their government is exploiting them. In their country, they only have two classes: rich and very poor. American citizens have to support these people. If something is not done soon to stop this invasion, the well is going to run dry. Money for wars and illegals will create more taxes on the public, and the USA will run out of money. The only way to slow down this tide is to refuse to give welfare benefits to any illegal. Tell them to go back to their country, and let them support their own people. We are not trying to be mean; we are trying to keep our country from going bankrupt. If politicians would have the guts to pass this law, maybe it would stem the tide. If the illegals heard that there were no free goodies, they might change their minds about coming here.

On the other hand, many Democrats want them to come here, so they get the illegals to vote to keep them in power. Obama and his gang are scheming now to give these illegals amnesty just for votes. This way, the Dummycrats will have a lock on the next election. Wake up, America; do not let this happen!

Rick Roberts, the radio commentator in San Diego, California, has said that we are three or four flushes away from going down the drain. Michael Savage, a radio talk show host, tells it like it is. Our politicians are weak and afraid to speak up. Mostly, it's the politicians who are against this country who are doing most of the talking. If the veterans of World War II and other wars had not fought for our freedom, these people, who show their ignorance, would be marching to the Nazi goose-step.

Maybe before I pass on, I can help America stay American. I think, as an American, we have been good to all the people who have come to this country. They work hard, and they get ahead in business and their lives. I do not have anything against them. In fact, I admire them for their foresight to see that they can accomplish the American dream.

The other day I spoke to an illegal Mexican. He told me he had been working in the United States for the last fifteen years. I asked him if his company deducted payroll taxes from his check. He said yes. I asked if he had a Social Security card. He responded no. I asked him how his company could take out Social Security deductions without his having a Social Security card. He did not know. He works for a small landscaping company that kept these deductions without telling him about it. He was afraid to report them because he is illegal. I guess that is the price he has to pay to keep the job.

There is much more corruption than meets the eye. I drove this man home one day and saw that he lives in a crowded ghetto, in an apartment that was only one large room. He pays $750 a month so that he, his wife, their six-year-old daughter, and their sixth-month-old baby can live in one room. Slumlords have no conscience. This man did a couple minor jobs for me at my home. I paid him handsomely because I knew he could use the money. This country has a problem: Here was a hard-working illegal who has never taken any money from our society, yet he will be put in the same category with all the illegals that prey on our welfare system.

We had all kinds of disasters in 2005: tsunamis, hurricanes, floods, earthquakes. Uncle Sam sends money to help the victims of these disasters. Instead, we should send clothes, food, and other essentials that are needed but not money; the politicians just steal it. The American public has to foot the bill all the time. Illegals come into this country and get welfare money, free education, and free medical. If refused, they get a lawyer who demands their rights. The only rights they have is a one-way ticket back to where they came from. Don't the do-nothing politicians realize that they are making it very easy for terrorists to get into this country? All they care about is getting votes to stay in power. They will regret the day a terrorist gets an A-bomb and blows up millions of people. These terrorists are bent on killing us. They do not care if they get killed.

There are leaders all over the world who are power-crazy, greedy, and do not care if their people get killed in a war. The people on earth were supposedly civilized many years ago. With all the murders, stealing, and lying nowadays, it makes me wonder if humanity has learned anything. The leaders of the terrorists install their propaganda into the heads of their young people. They tell them to become a suicide bomber and blow themselves and innocent people to death by assuring them that they will go to heaven. Why don't the leaders want to go to heaven? They are slick; they make the dummies do it. I'd like to ask the terrorists: Why do your leaders tell you to commit yourself to death? Do they not want to go to heaven with seventy virgins? They are pretty shrewd. They have idiots killing for them, instead of doing the dirty work themselves. Our government should be spreading this message to the Arab population in newspapers and television. We should use the propaganda that they are stupid for being suicide bombers for their leaders. This should be pounded into their heads daily, with no letup.

We have a problem in this country that is very difficult to solve. One thing is sure: we are getting overcrowded, in our schools and with all the traffic. We have to stem the tide, not only of Mexicans but of all other immigrants. That is up to our do-nothing politicians. All they care about is cuddling up to these people, giving them more goodies, and getting their votes at the expense of the taxpayer. The only way to stop this is to call your senators and congressmen so they will get the message.

ON PROTESTORS AND PATRIOTISM

The other day I heard on the radio that a mother of a soldier was blaming President Bush for the death of her son, who was killed in Iraq. To start with, her son volunteered for service. In World War II, the five Sullivan brothers were killed when their ship went down in the Pacific. Over a half a million men were killed in World War II. Many were drafted. I did not hear any mothers blaming FDR. People must understand that war is not pleasant. Sometimes, we wonder if it is worth it. Freedom is precious. We have an enemy that wants to destroy us and our children. We have to fight the enemy, like it or not. Those countries are jealous of our lifestyle. They have their people propagandized with that bull about going to heaven if they blow themselves up and kill other people with the explosion. I do not see any of their leaders blowing themselves up. They are too slick to fall for that nonsense. It may take a few years, but we will survive. We are on the right side.

Today, the remarks made by people and some politicians make me ill. In World War II, anyone who made remarks against the war would be put in jail or sentenced to death for treason. War is a dirty business. People are killed, soldiers die, just to give freedom to the loud mouths that we have in this country. There was plenty of criticism of our war in Iraq.

If you want to start criticizing, let us go back to World War II. I am veteran of that war. We could have criticized President Roosevelt about the way he misled the American people to get in the war. We knew this, but the American people are always willing to help people who are oppressed. Over 500,000 sailors and soldiers died to keep this country free. We were told to hate and kill the Germans and Japanese. After the war, what did we do? We helped Germany and Japan to an economic recovery of great proportions. We did not criticize our government, and there was plenty of room to do so. We did not punish the civilians who were innocent of the crimes of their dictators. After a few years, we traded with those countries, buying cars, etc. It helped our economy, too. That is why people in the United States have a better life today. Practically everyone owns a car and has money to spend. Children go to college. When I was young, only the wealthy could send their children to college. So, ignorant protesters should count their blessings and keep their mouths shut. They should learn many things before they protest.

Some of our people want investigations on the way in which we treat enemy prisoners. How about investigations into how our people had their heads cut off? Wake up, America! If events keep going the way they are, there is going to be a revolution in this country. This will create another Hitler. There are too many people pecking away at our values. Our lawyers are overeager to defend these morons who continuously attack our way of life, just to make more money. Some of these spoiled traitors who have it too easy in this country should be put in the military. Then, they'd find out how it is to live in a foxhole with water covering your feet, not knowing if you would be killed, or on a ship, never knowing if a torpedo or a plane would crash into them. Radicals will say there should be no war. If it were not for the efforts of the American people and military in World War II, the Korean War, and Vietnam, Americans would be speaking German or Asian. If we are not alert, we will be speaking Arabic soon.

Remember that the veterans who sacrificed in our nation's past wars received only a medal. The morons of today are receiving the freedom to shoot off their ignorant mouths. Just think how our military is sacrificing in Iraq, with that desert heat, etc., wondering when a suicide bomber is going to try to kill them. I am very proud of them. As a veteran myself, I can feel for them. These morons who have it comfortable can only criticize the war. They keep saying that President Bush lied to them to get into the war. How about President Clinton? He said that Saddam Hussein was trying to improve on biological weapons and atomic bombs. Do these people forget what they have done to us? They killed over two hundred U.S. Marines in a bombing in Lebanon during the Reagan administration. They bombed the USS *Cole*, killing several sailors. In 1993, they bombed the World Trade Center in New York, wounding hundreds of people. We still sat on our hands. Then in 2001, 9/11 happened, killing nearly three thousand Americans.

What are these morons waiting for—an atomic bomb to explode in one of our cities, killing millions of people, including themselves? How many more of these incidents must happen before Americans start to believe that we are defending ourselves against these radicals? Maybe they are waiting for them to cut a few more heads off. We did the right thing by invading Iraq. We stalled Al-Qaeda, because after 9/11, they felt they could do anything to the United States. Our government did not do its homework. It is still not too late to use diplomacy and money to make a deal to keep all sides happy.

I see protesters on television waving foreign flags, not U.S. flags, and I hear about

schools preventing the display of anything patriotic, such as students wearing anything resembling the American flag. My two brothers and I, along with other veterans, fought to preserve our freedom and our flag. I become enraged when I think of school administrators who succumb to so-called political correctness—that students who come to school with an American flag on their jackets should be criticized. It is unbelievable. Why is it that in our own country, we have to be scared to display our patriotism? We are not going to take this disgrace anymore. We are going to take our country back via Rick Robert's Radio Talk Show (1-800-760-5362). All politicians are invited to call anytime between the hours of 9 AM and 4 PM, Pacific time, Monday through Friday. Any other inquiries are welcome.

On Lawyers and the Law

The lawyers in this country are a legal mafia. They should be known as ALM—American Legal Mafia. (That is a phrase they would not appreciate very much.) People go to court and win an award of five million dollars, for example, but end up with one million after the lawyers' fees. That is because of the outrageous fees the lawyers charge. They get away with this because Congress won't put a cap on legal fees. That is why trial lawyers disliked President Bush. He attempted to do just that, but Congress tabled the bill. I am not condemning all lawyers, but if you have had any experience with them, you probably understand what I mean. Money is the root of all evil. I am not a very religious man, but the world would be better off without greed. Fifty years from now, we might go back to the barter system, but I will not be around to see it happen. I am having some experience with lawyers now who charge six hundred dollars an hour. I said to one of them, "When I was a young boy, I read the Bible in school. I read that Jesus Christ walked on water. Before I pay six hundred dollars an hour to a lawyer, I want to see if he can walk on water without a life preserver."

The world is sure different today than when I was growing up. In my time, if someone committed murder—and especially if he admitted it—he was sent to the electric chair. Today, murderers are given lawyers to defend them for free. They stay on death row for twenty years or more, waiting for their lawyers to come up with a feeble excuse to get a pardon. In the meantime, the victim gets buried and the family has to pay taxes for the murderer to stay in jail. During World War II, no one would dare speak against the war or the government. They would be labeled a traitor, and it could bring on a harsh penalty.

They say everyone has civil rights. What about the victims who are buried six feet under? What rights do they have? This country is being led down the road to total disaster; the public must wake up. I get very angry when I think of all the boys who fought in World War II, Korea, and Vietnam and died to preserve our freedom. Now, women and men are fighting in Iraq, and we have people putting them down with their sob stories about how we treat enemy prisoners. They should see the ugly scenes we saw in World War II—U.S. prisoners with their ribs showing from being almost starved to death. In World War II, if we caught a spy, we would supply the man with the electric chair—period. Now, the terrorists know we are soft, so they have no fear. The country had better wise up before terrorists blow us to pieces. I do not understand the American public; they hear from radio and television commentators, like Rush Limbaugh, Sean Hannity, and Bill O'Reilly. Michael Savage is the most outspoken on terrorism. I give him credit for alerting his listeners to the problems we have. I do not understand how some of our people, including politicians, can talk against our nation. They do not realize how lucky they are to live in this country.

On Health Care

Have you had an experience in the hospital where you had surgery, and afterward, your primary doctor peeks his head in the door, says good mourning, and then you are charged a hundred dollars a day for his visit? Then, the hospital triples your bill so you can pay for the parasites who get free medical attention? I always wonder about doctors because a personal friend of mine became a doctor. He had an office in the neighborhood. I said, "Doctor, Mrs. Caruso comes to your office every week. What is wrong with her?"

He said, "Nothing. I give her an injection every week."

"If there is nothing wrong, why the needle?" I asked.

"All that is in the needle is plain water," he answered. "It is all psychological with her; it just makes her feel better."

For some people, if their doctor does not give them a pill or an antibiotic, they think he is not a good doctor. Really, our immune system does 85 percent of the healing on its own.

My son is a doctor, but he is in research. Researchers use their knowledge in trying to find cures for diseases. I am currently involved with my other son, Anthony, in biotech. I am the CFO of the company. We work hard to keep the company alive, trying to find cures for diseases like tuberculosis, diabetes, and malaria. We more or less have to beg the government for grants. We've also invested plenty of our personal money in this cause.

My younger brother lost his wife at the age of forty-six years, due to cancer. He also had a son who had a kidney problem at the age of twelve and had to go on dialysis, three days a week, for twenty-two years. He passed away at the age of thirty-four. Twenty years later, my brother had kidney failure. He has been on dialysis for the past six months. He and other people are suffering with diseases, yet in the scientific world, we have to plead for money to find help for millions of people.

When I was a young man, I lost three uncles on my dad's side of the family to tuberculosis. Later on in years, my dad also died from TB. So, in a way, I am committed to this cause. I know the dangers of this disease firsthand. There are many ways to become infected: people coughing close to you, eating in a public place that has unwashed utensils, using a towel onto which an infected person has coughed. My concern is the illegals coming into this country undetected. They are entering without being examined for TB or other diseases. If one gets a job in a restaurant and coughs on a glass or a utensil, it would be very easy to infect others. I know from experience the precautions my mother and brothers had to take to prevent their acquiring the disease. I think that if my uncles had taken the precautions we did, they would have lived a longer life. My dad outlived his brothers, but he tried everything to survive. He spent several months in a TB sanatorium. He was treated at the sanatorium with a new medication that science discovered called streptomycin. It was very helpful. He lived several more years with a healthy life.

When I recollect my uncles, I wonder if they got the proper care. They were poor, and I guess when one became ill with TB, he passed it on to his brothers. They probably slept three in a bed, not knowing what precautions to take. So, they probably infected each other. That is why they died at a young age. When I was young, I wondered why they were dying so frequently. When my dad showed signs of the disease, we made it our business to have him checked by a physician. He told my mother the pitfalls of not taking precautions to prevent infections. We took stringent steps to keep from getting infected—using separate glasses, dishes, towels, etc. When my dad's condition worsened, he had to go to a sanatorium for several months. That is when he was given the drug to neutralize his condition. We were grateful that science had discovered a drug that enabled him to live many more years.

People do not realize that we are all at risk. Today, people are slipping into this country by the millions without being screened for disease. Just think if some of these illegals have TB, and gets a job as a bartender, and squeezes a lime in your drink and drops it in your glass, and has the TB germ on his fingers. If your immune system is low, you can become infected. Also, if they are smokers and they cough in their hands, they might think that it is a cigarette cough, not knowing they are spreading germs on your glass, cup, or dish. There are so many ways you can catch these germs. I know I have been very cautious all my life. Our scientists are working diligently, trying to find a vaccine to prevent the most common infections.

So far, research and development have been very expensive. Government grants have become very scarce since the Iraq war began and with recent money problems in the economy. I am determined to help find a cure for these diseases in memory of my dad and my uncles. It is tragic that they had to die so young. I do not want this happen to other young people. It is my hope that we can accomplish this in my lifetime. Our scientists have made very promising inroads in their experiments, but money has become a critical issue. That is why I am pleading to the public for donations to further research for all biotech companies.

As you know, our government has sent millions of our tax dollars to Africa to feed and help the people there to be cured from tuberculosis, malaria, etc. Right now, in Ethiopia, there are millions of people, especially children, who are starving. We send money, and the corrupt politicians keep it. In the meantime, children are infected by disease. We should send vaccines that cure people, not send money. If we discover the vaccine, as I am very confident that we will, that will save many lives. To give to our cause will make you feel good that you are part of helping unfortunate people. Please consider it.

On the Drug Problem

What is going to happen to our society in the near future if we don't solve the drug problem? The other day, I heard that four young men, between the ages of twenty-one and twenty-three, died from overdoses of drugs. I am convinced that this generation of young people is really ignorant and that they do not realize that drugs will kill them prematurely. I researched these deaths and found that the young men came from wealthy families. Five of my grandchildren are between the ages of fifteen and twenty-two years. I speak to them frequently, telling them about the dangers of drugs. I learned from one of my grandchildren that some parents now have their children tested for drugs, but children have ways to foil the tests by putting some kind of drops in the urine to keep the tests negative. Now, however, the medical profession has a new procedure—they can test for drug use by testing the person's hair. Children cannot get around that procedure.

Are we headed for a generation of drug addicts? My generation never had this problem because we never heard about drugs. There might have been minor problems with alcoholism, but of all my friends that I grew up with, I do not remember any becoming an alcoholic. I do remember that all of us starting to smoke at a young age. We did not know about lung cancer in that era. When medical professionals started to talk about the link between smoking and cancer, I immediately stopped smoking. That was over forty years ago. I believe that's one reason why I am still living at an old age.

Our government is responsible for the health of the public. The greed is in Washington to collect taxes on cigarettes, so they can get their hands on more money. Why do they not ban cigarettes? Are they afraid it might start a black market selling of these cancer sticks? Our government could stop the flow of drugs if it wanted to do so. Instead of sending American troops to Iraq, put them on our borders and inspect every car and truck thoroughly before it enters this country.

ON RELIGION

I heard on the radio that the pope wants immunity from divulging any information about priests committing inappropriate acts with children. I am Catholic, and I've always felt that the Church is archaic in its rules. Priests and nuns should be allowed to marry. They are human. This would eliminate 95 percent of the lewd acts committed by priests.

In the end, it's all about money. The Church says to refrain from using birth control. Some Catholics have fifteen children in their families. That is a more customers for the Church. The Mormons have their people donate 10 percent of their salaries weekly to their church. The rabbis have their way to keep their flock in line.

I do not understand why, when I ask a Jewish person what nationality he is, he will say, "I am Jewish." That is not a nationality; that is a religion. If I were to ask a non-Jew, he would answer Irish American or Italian-American, etc. I once asked a Jewish person his nationality, and he said he did not know.

Most of us believe in God. All religions try to keep us in line for their own gain. The way things are going today, they are not very successful. Crime is up, drugs are running rampant, and there seems to be no end to this trend. I hope that my six grandchildren are able to live a better world than we have now.

We know that some of these religions help people and support causes, such as taking take care of orphans. So why do we send billions of dollars to foreign countries every year? This money does not get to the people who need it. The politicians keep it. For example, in Africa, people are starving by the millions because of their corrupt governments. They also are victims to malaria, tuberculosis, HIV, etc. Our biotech lab is working diligently on malaria and TB, although we struggle to get funding. Bill Gates has given millions of dollars to research. Some large companies have received millions for research cures for these diseases.

Our company has given some of these large companies data that is very helpful for making vaccines for these diseases, but these companies do not want to give us any advance money so we can continue our projects. They have millions and are not willing to give us any to carry on. They are interested in our research, but whoever controls the funding is very short-sighted. We are not looking for large amounts of money, only enough to keep our projects going.

On Modern Culture

As a teenager, when I met a friend, I would say hiya, or I would nod. Today, kids seem to use their fists to greet each other. At a football or baseball game, spectators give each other the "high five" after every play. I've also noticed that people stand up for the entire game, blocking the view of the people behind them—no one sits in their seats. At one game, I went to buy two hot dogs and two sodas for my son and me.

"What do I owe you?" I asked the girl who served me.

"Twenty-one dollars," she answered.

I put my hands up in the air and said to her, "Put your gun down!"

She laughed and said, "I only work here." I know everything is more expensive these days, but I could not help thinking that when my dad took me to a ball game, a hot dog cost five cents, a hamburger was ten cents, and a soda was a nickel. That was many moons ago.

Today, the young generation does not seem to know what respect means. In my generation, respect was number one on the agenda. There was no such punishment as two minutes in the corner, and no attitudes like, "If you touch me, I will turn you in to the authorities." Just to respond to your parents in a negative way was a big no-no. That also went for your teachers and any other adults.

Today, some boys wear pants that are too large and hang down, with their bare butts showing. Their parents should throw away their clothes and not let them leave the house unless they reform. Some girls get tattoos on their butts and walk around as if they are proud of their appearance. Maybe some parents should pay more attention to their children.

Today's slang is different from what it was in my day. In my time, when someone looked good and did something intelligent, the remark was that he or she was "sharp." Today, the kids say "cool." I thought "cool" had to do with the weather. Today, when I hear some African Americans speak, I sometimes don't know what they are saying. They say "man." The reason for this is that years ago, especially in the South, people would call blacks "boy." The blacks resented that term and would reply, "I am a man, not a boy." It took almost fifty years for the term "boy" to be removed from street language.

On Modern Politics

When I was young, I always thought congressmen, senators, and all other politicians were honest. They cannot be. Our system has made it very difficult for anyone without sufficient funds to run for office. The costs are huge for campaign advertising. Unless the candidates are wealthy, they have no choice but to go to their friends and ask for money to run their campaigns. When they get elected, they owe their sponsors. Then the corruption starts. Elected officials are told to vote for certain bills that their sponsors have interest in. The sponsors make millions, and the politicians' greed gets activated when they wants several million for themselves. That is where some of our taxes go. Every few years, politicians want to raise their salaries. They want the public to think they are underpaid. That is a farce. If the salary is so bad, why do they spend millions trying to get elected? We condemn other countries for corruption, but they do not hide their practices. Most of our politicians try to show the public that they are honorable. In the meantime, they keep the public confused with our outrageous tax code. Written by Congress, it is more than ten thousand pages. Congress wants to keep us thinking that the rich get all the tax breaks, that the wealthy pay most of the taxes. They can fool some of the people some of the time, but not all of the people all of the time.

Maybe someday we will get honest politicians to do the right thing. There are many discrepancies to be corrected. As usual, it is all about desire for unearned money. Farmers are making more money now than in all of history. Still, today they get millions of dollars in subsidies. The slick politician pulls strings and gets a deal for millions in taxpayers' money for his friends, and then he is tempted to get his kickback. This goes on year after year. Why don't they run campaigns for two weeks only? That would put an end to this underground money.

Billions of dollars in taxpayers' money has been wasted on a war in Iraq; plus, many of our young people have been killed. This war could last twenty-five years or more at this pace. Terrorists are fanatics, just like the Japanese were in World War II. They are willing to blow themselves up for Allah. They are brainwashed.

My suggestion is this: Of the 160,000 troops in Iraq, deploy 100,000 back to the United States and leave 60,000 in Iraq. Of those 60,000, put 10,000 troops to guard the oil fields and the other 50,000 to continue instructing the Iraqi army on how to defend themselves from the terrorists. If Iran decides to cross the border into Iraq, that is an act of war. We have had two aircraft carriers sitting in the bay for the last five years with one hundred jet fighter bombers. Our planes can destroy their troops in short order. We should also give Iran a warning that more destruction will come to Iran if they do not behave. They only understand one thing: the iron fist. That seems to keep all these dictators at bay.

In the Iraq war, our government made plenty of mistakes. After 9/11, the enemy felt that they could get away with anything. We had no choice but to confront them. What our government did not understand is that the enemy understands only one thing: *brute force*. Our government should notify the Iraqi civilian population to vacate certain cities. Then our air force should pulverize those cities. Our enemies understand that better than diplomacy. Japan had the same attitude until we dropped two atomic bombs on their country. Soldiers in Iraq have the hardest fight on their hands. They are fighting a hidden enemy. Our government did not do its homework before entering the Iraq war. People in Iraq have been fighting each other for thousands of years. They were taught to hate Western culture. The only way we could have changed some issues is with money. We already have spent over two hundred billion dollars, and that cost is still climbing. If I was an advisor, this what I would have suggested as a way to spend that much money: I would have our CIA contact some members of Saddam Hussein's guard and promise them two billion dollars now and two billion after they assassinate him. Then, get to the leaders of the Shiites and the Sunnis and offer them five billion dollars each to promote peace among themselves. We would still have 186 billion dollars left. That is quite a bit with which to do more bribery. I know this comment is after the fact, but if our government would approach the leaders of the Shiites and Sunnis and offer them a deal, I am sure they would accept. Remember, we can save billions of dollars of taxpayers' money. What do we have to lose if we try this approach? It is going to cost many billions more before the end is in sight. The new Iraq government is only window dressing. They have no real power. The terrorists have made a mockery of them. We have to get Shiites and Sunnis on our side with money. That would cause a split between Iraq and Osama Bin Laden. The terrorists would be disillusioned with this deal. They would try to get in on the money. How do you think Saddam Hussein kept his power? He supplied his gang with money to keep him in power. The old adage is "Money talks and bullshit walks." This is the only way we can get out of this mess. People might say that they would blackmail us for more money. While we are there, if we do not see change, we are back to square one. Nothing ventured, nothing gained. Why not give it a try? And if it works, our troops would not be in harm's way.

A Middle Eastern person told me once, "If you put ten Arabs in a room to work out a business deal, they would kill each other." I do not believe that. Put enough money in the mix, and things will happen. Put ten Jews in a room, and believe me, there would be a deal. They like doing business; that's their nature.

Barack Obama and Hillary Clinton argue, but I do not see too much difference in their agendas. Hillary wants to give health care to everyone in the country. She will have the government take more taxes out of our paychecks, denying workers the funds they need to educate their children. Obama has a plan to reduce costs for health care. Does he want doctors and nurses to take a pay reduction? On the Republican side, we have John McCain, who seems to have lost his memory that he was against the Bush's tax cuts. He forgot what he said about amnesty for illegals, etc. We have to forgive him because he is a half of a Democrat anyway. Keep in mind, I was writing this book before the election.

Today, our politicians recommend that some citizens depend on the government for support. That makes these people lazy, and it makes it easy for them not to have any ambition to better themselves. Greedy politicians only want their votes. I do not want to take sides on this subject, but the Democrats seem to be the party that encourages this agenda. They use that same old line: tax the rich and give to the poor. Eighty percent of the so-called poor need to get off their butts and try to make their lives more successful, instead of waiting for government handouts. Unfortunately, Barack Obama is promising them more money at the end of the rainbow— this would be at the expense of the middle class, who will have more money taken out of their paychecks. They are struggling now to pay their mortgages, children's education, high fuel taxes, food prices, etc. The slick politicians will say that only the rich will be taxed, but anyone who grosses over $60,000 a year will get hit with higher taxes. Take a family of four that has two children to send to college, a mortgage, and costs for fuel, food, etc. The so-called rich have many ways to divert some of their money, so the politicians have to tax the middle class more. Obama is going to give everyone who goes to college a $4,000 deduction. Big deal. Tuition often starts at $25,000 or more. Guess who is going to pay for the reduction? You guessed right: the middle class.

Nowadays, young people want to lie back and have the government give them handouts. Years ago, I was in small-claims court, and a young woman was complaining to the judge that although her college tuition paid for by the government, the government would not pay her for her taxi fare to get to school. The judge asked her if there was a bus stop nearby. She admitted that there was but that she did not like waiting five or ten minutes for the bus to arrive.

Today, some people are spoiled rotten. Everyone has to pay more taxes to keep these vultures satisfied. The politicians cater to these people just to get their votes. All the people who donate money to politicians' campaigns are looking for change. But all the change we will see is more taxes and more socialism. Everyone will have to work harder to support the lazy people who look to the government for handouts. During the Depression of the 1930s, the government had a program for young men call the CCC: Civilian Conservation Corps. They would labor on clearing roads, forests, etc. They made a little money to help their families get through the rough times, and they had a place to sleep, even if it was tents. This was much better than handouts because it gave people self-respect.

Some of the so-called poor sit on their butts and get checks from the government, while we suckers work hard and have our paychecks hit for these lazy people. The welfare bureaucracy running the current system is in favor of the status quo. There have been hundreds of scandals, with people giving kickbacks to these government workers. I spent forty years in the ghetto with my import business, and many employees would tell me what goes on in these areas. I do not know if everyone is familiar with the welfare system. For every dollar spent on welfare, eight-seven cents is taken out for administration costs—unbelievable, but it is true. Maybe someday we will have honest people running the welfare system. If the government would investigate scandals, maybe we would have honesty in our current system.

We have the same problem in Iraq. We spend billions to help that country, which is rich in oil. We should be getting oil free from them. Instead, they are getting financed beyond their dreams. They will never say that their country is stable. They want us to stay forever. The only thing that will become stable is their treasury. They will never admit to that. As Uncle "Sap" keeps giving; they will keep taking. In the meantime, the American public will keep paying outrages price for fuel and other commodities. Mexico has billions of barrels of oil. Why doesn't our government tell them to supply us with oil, particularly as we are supporting millions of their illegals on welfare? Their oil would be more economical, because they could build a pipeline directly into California. That makes sense, but it will not happen, because they have to protect these conglomerates.

We are complaining about fuel prices. President Bush had to go to Saudi Arabia and beg the king for more oil to slow down the price gouging. Without the United States, the Saudis could not sell most of their oil. Bush should have bluffed the king and said that the United States was going to cut way back on the use of oil. To start with, we should sacrifice one day a month, on Saturday or Sunday, and stay home. There are 136 million cars on the road and still growing. Except for the people who drive to work on Saturdays and Sundays, the rest of us could stay home for that one day, and let's estimate that it could leave about thirty-six million cars on the road on a weekend day. That would cut back five hundred million gallons of gas. Additionally, we would save at least five gallons of gas each.

If the king of Saudi Arabia thinks he will sell the excess oil to China, he better take another look. There are plenty people in China still riding bicycles. Also, in the United States, there should be a limit of two cars per household. Remember, every year more sixteen- or seventeen-year-olds get cars. That's millions more dollars in gas consumption. When gas goes to seven dollars per gallon, maybe we will wake up. For sure, the oil-producing companies do not want the price go down. Our oil companies are making more money now than ever before.

Our federal government and state governments are enjoying the taxes we pay on the purchase of gas. When gas prices rise, it takes two weeks for that gas to be processed. But oil companies raise the price ten cents a gallon overnight. The gas stations rush to post the new price on their gas signs and add a little more to the price. I just cannot believe that with our technology, we cannot produce cars that do not need gas. Back in 1969, we put a man on the moon. Now, we cannot produce cars that run without gas? Maybe the oil companies and our government have something to do with this. Instead of being leaders, we have become beggars to the Middle East countries that only want our money-and despise us.

The Environmental Protection Agency nuts do not want us to drill for oil in Alaska—it might affect the caribou. The poor animals might have to jump over the pipelines. There are thousands of miles of uninhabited land up there. The do-gooders have to complain about something to keep their jobs. Also, global warming is more bull about melting ice in the Arctic. They took pictures in July, when it was warm all over the Northern Hemisphere. Al Gore made plenty of money with this phony act. I spoke to a scientist who claims that global warming is false. They cannot announce it publicly, because it is not politically correct, and the company for whom they work for might release them of their job. This is a cycle that has gone on for millions of years. In fact, the scientists say we are heading for a cooler period.

Barack Obama says he is going to change the system. The only change he is going to make is bringing in his pals on the continuous corruption. I have been watching our political system for over sixty years. Nothing changes, except the new faces that get into the political circle. The real challenge is our new, younger politicians who are on the extreme left; they are trying to run our lives. They want a government-run health system, economic control to supposedly prevent global warming, no drilling for oil, etc. Little by little, they are taking away our freedoms. I heard that no one is allowed to build any more fast-food outlets in Los Angeles, California. Presumably, this is to protect the obese. Bull—they want to take away our freedom.

America, wake up and vote these leftist politicians out of office. When I think of all the veterans who sacrificed to preserve our freedom, and then I watch these anti-Americans doing their best to propagandize our citizens against our principles, it makes my blood boil. They call us racist. Racism has been going on for thousands of years, and it will continue for many more thousands of years. It cannot be helped. People discriminate against each other all the time. When I think back fifty years ago, I remember that the Jewish people would always vote for a Democrat, regardless of who was running. I think it has to do with religion. Republicans were known to be WASPs (White Anglo-Saxon Protestants). That left Jews, Italians, African Americans, and others out of the mainstream. That was many years ago. The Democratic Party saw an opportunity to seize upon a theory to benefit their party. They told non-WASPs, "Look, they have all the money, and you are poor." The Democrats have been using that line for seventy-five years. All I know is that there are many billionaires who are Democrats. What puzzles me is why the African Americans vote 98 percent Democrat. Abe Lincoln was a Republican and had the Union fight to free the slaves. The Civil Rights Act that was passed in the 1960s had more Republicans vote in favor of it than Democrats. Still, they vote for Democrats. They have been so brainwashed that they only vote one way. The Jewish people still hold a grudge against the WASPs; that is probably a religious matter. Religion should not enter politics. Vote for candidates that seem honest, regardless of the party. I know it is hard, because there are many legal gangsters in DC. Maybe someday we will get politicians who try to help all people, rather than the corruption club they have now, which consists of both Democrats and Republicans.

The media annoys me when a Republican gets caught in wrongdoing. He is blasted for weeks. In contrast, when a Democrat is caught pulling a fast one, you hear about it for one or two days. For example, just recently Senator Dodd (D-Conn.) got a deal in which his mortgage was reduced by $80,000. How about the congressman who was caught by the FBI with over $100,000 in cash in his freezer that he made taking bribes? We heard a few mumbles. Yet he has not been charged—again, a Democrat. The Democrats have the media in their back pockets.

I cannot understand why some politicians in DC are they against drilling for oil. The excuse they give is that it negatively impacts the environment. Bull. There is more to it than that. I think it is some kind of deal that we do not know about. Does it ever enter their minds that if the Middle East countries put an embargo on oil shipments to the United States, especially if Al-Qaeda gets control, they can bring us down to our knees? We will have no transportation, resulting in massive interruptions in producing and distributing products. We can use our reserve for six months— then what? Go to war with the whole Arab world? We should be working feverishly on alternate fuels. The government should give grants to companies that are working on these fuels. That would reduce the need for fossil fuel, and prices would be cheaper than gasoline. That makes sense. But for some reason, the government wants to keep the public off balance all the time. I guess the only way to get something going is to go to DC and lobby like the rest are doing. Then, promise some politician that if he or she helps to push a bill though a committee, he or she will be compensated. That is the way it is. I guess the old adage is still true: it's not what you know, it is who you know. We are spending money by the billions, Democrats and Republicans alike. We are printing money by the billions, as if printing paper equals creating wealth. The day of reckoning is coming. It will be a very sad day.

Today, we are at a dangerous juncture, where too many nations have the atomic bombs that can annihilate the entire human race. Today's hydrogen bombs are one hundred times more powerful than the atomic bombs that were dropped on Japan in 1945. The only weapon our politicians can use is diplomacy. You cannot threaten other countries into submission because most countries now have the bomb. From now on, our diplomatic corps better brush up on how to confuse other countries with our propaganda.

Maybe we are trying to influence other countries with our democracy propaganda. Some countries do not care about democracy. All they care about is survival. Uncle Sam gets involved and gives away billions in taxpayer money. That money should stay here and give relief to U.S. taxpayers. Our politicians in DC want to meddle in other countries' problems. For example, Russia has problems with Georgia. Why do we have to have troops on their border? If Russia put troops on the Mexican border, we would not like it very much. That is how wars start. Russia has the right to claim their own land. We are trying to influence the world. History has proven that there is not one country that can control the entire planet.

On Economics and the Bailouts

I really get agitated when I see the politicians make fools out of the American public. Congress voted against the bailout bill, and what happened? The Senate came up with its own version, with a few minor changes. The FDIC will insure your CDs up to $250,000. If you have a CD in the bank for $100,000, all you are covered for is the $100,000. The Stimulis Bill includes a bill with 450 pages. I will bet that not one single senator has read it, including Barack Obama and John McCain. They take us for fools and slip anything they want in the bill. Then, they have the audacity to put Senator Harry Reid on television, praising Senator Dodd for his work on the bill. He is the main culprit who bragged that Freddie Mac and Fannie May were in great financial shape. They were part of the scheme to force banks to give loans to unqualified buyers. The speculators, who mostly did not put money down, were in the majority. When the home prices fell, they walked away from their loans. They did not lose anything. Our corrupt politicians, Barney Frank and Christopher Dodd, encouraged the lenders to make loans backed by Freddie and Fannie because they were getting kickbacks. The CEO who retired from FM received $90 million for six years' service. The FBI should investigate these corrupt people. The few that I mentioned are not the only ones. I guarantee you there are many more politicians involved. Yet the IRS will persecute people who cheat for little amounts.

There are too many problems in the world today. Our leaders are influenced by special interests. They are too occupied with these corrupt politicians and have no time for the general public. We send billions of dollars overseas to foreign countries that are jealous of us and despise our country. If those billions stayed in this country, our leaders could do great things for the American people, instead of overtaxing everything they can think of. They could make it more economical for our children to go to college, instead of the outrages prices we pay now.

Our leaders could put money into states that are on the brink of budget collapse. This would reduce sales taxes and real estate taxes. This would ease the pressure on the public. They could remove the death tax, which is double taxation. They will not do it because it makes sense. They could start a federal lottery that would bring millions of dollars a day to the cause of lower taxes. Maybe someday we will get leaders in DC with some brains and good ideas—but do not bet on it.

The news keeps repeating that we are in a recession. All I know is that every stadium that has a football or baseball team seems full to the brim, despite the very high ticket prices. The only commodity that is receding in price is gasoline, for now. The price is still too expensive. Other items, such as food and energy, are increasing in price. During the Depression, merchants would do anything to get people to buy their merchandise. They would extend credit for weeks. They knew people were honest but did not have money to pay immediately. They knew in the end they would receive their money. There was honor in those days. I guess corruption did not exist because of the sacristy of money. We old-timers know the pain of entering the long and terrible Depression of the 1930s. The only good thing about the Depression was that food and all other products were very affordable. It was supply and demand. We had too much supply, and the population was down. That made prices stay down. Today, the population keeps increasing daily. Therefore, prices will remain expensive. That causes hardship on low-income families. Today, the United States is able to grow enough food to feed over three hundred million people. We should be thankful; some countries are not able to feed their own population. If the United States sent food instead of money to impoverished nations, we would make friends when the people knew it was sent by America. We need the small farmers to keep the competition against the corporate farmers who get subsidies from our government. That puts them in a position to control prices on the food we need. Everything in this world is about money. Pride and honesty have disappeared from our society. Politics has become dirty. Politicians should have term limits. This way, they would have less time to get infected with the shady deals that go on every day with our taxpayers' money. I still say that the Freddie Mac and Fannie Mae scandal should be thoroughly investigated. The public knows which politicians were involved and the CEOs who stole millions.

Our country is in a financial mess that will not be easy to resolve. I was talking to my banker the other day, and he told me that this mess started back when Bill Clinton was president. He ordered all banks and lending companies not to redline minorities and lower-income people from getting loans so they could borrow money to buy a house. None of these people was qualified to buy a home. The banks were forced to go along with it. The minorities that were qualified jumped in because it hardly cost them any money to own a house. The smart banks that recognized this farce sold their mortgages to the big lenders, like Countrywide, AIG,

Lehman Brothers, and Freddie Mac and Fannie Mae. The greed set in. They thought that when these people defaulted on their payments, they would foreclose and sell the houses for a handsome profit. The real estate market was very strong at that time. When interest rates increased, the people who borrowed this money could not afford to pay and had to give up their homes. The speculators did not care. They hardly put up any money at all and left the homes. Meantime, the real estate market lost much of its value. The big lenders were left with billions of dollars of uncollectible debts. Some greedy banks that held on to the loans were caught up into this mess. Now, the government has to rescue these lenders. Who is going to pay? The taxpayers—all because a politician wanted to play big shot with minorities and others, just to get their votes.

Did I say this country is in a financial bind? Large companies are going bankrupt, Congress is falling asleep on regulations, top corporate executives are doing shaky moves behind the scenes, and the government is bailing them out. They are getting large amounts of money for retirement pay that runs into millions of dollars. The investors lose their money and get ashes in their mouths. The CEOs should be put in jail for all the corrupt deals they made while running their companies. The public always has to take the brunt and pay more taxes. The Wall Street gangsters and the CEOs have put this country in great danger of a depression. Most of all, I blame our government for forcing the banks to give loans to unqualified buyers.

Last month, my brother Vince passed away. I flew to the East Coast to attend the services. I met with my nieces and one nephew and also met with some friends. This was my first visit in five years. I spoke with my sister-in-law. She was facing some financial difficulties because Vince had discontinued his insurance, as he could not afford the payments that were over $300 per month. He was a senior, and because of his age, the payments were excessive. The irony of this is that he canceled his policy only three months before his passing. His social security check arrived three days after his death. His widow had to return the check because he died a few days before the fifteenth of the month. This is how our government discriminates against seniors. Then, they put the widow through many difficulties to collect $255 for burial expenses. That amount never changed in sixty years. I want the government to show seniors how to pay for burial on $255. When a senator or congressman retires or passes on, their families receive the same millions that they were getting before. The government should at least let the family keep the last social security check because $255 is insufficient for burial costs. They should increase that amount to keep up with inflation. When a senior loses a mate that was on Social Security, they are given the disgraceful amount of $ 255, which could not cover a burial for a bird.

DC needs plenty of change to get rid of the corruption that goes on daily. Let the people get a break and lower taxes. That would put more money in their hands to enjoy with their families. I hope that someday this country will do what is right. Why does the public stand by while those corrupt crooks in Washington get away with raping the financial system? One year ago, Sen. Dodd said that Fannie May and Freddie Mac were making money when, all the while, he knew they were holding bad paper. His buddy, Congressman Barney Frank, chimed in with the same bull, and they kept taking money. We should have the FBI investigate all these corrupt politicians, in and out. The CEO of Freddie Mac was given ninety million dollars after he ran out on his job because he was afraid of a investigation.

These CEOs got outrageous severance bonuses. They should get jail terms. It was stupid to give Treasury Secretary Geithner $700 billion. He will take care of his buddies at Goldman Sachs, because he worked there. We should form a committee of people who are not politicians or Wall Street con artists, just honest men who have experience in their own businesses and have them look into the situation of companies like AIG, Merrill Lynch, and the others. The committee must not be hasty but should take a good look at each company's situation.

If banks and other lenders look hopeless, they claim that politicians in the Clinton administration and the Democratic Party forced them to give loans to unqualified buyers. The banks should have rebelled and protested. They all knew this was dangerous. They all sat on their hands, while the corrupt crooks had a field day. The Republicans made a meek revolt in Congress, but Democrats voted them down. I say, do not hand over a dime to Geithner until we get an honest opinion from an outside investigation. Bush, with his meek warnings, only gave the gangsters more arrogance to continue.

Money creates evil, but it also does good. The Japanese economy flourished for several decades. That was due to the change from their ancient customs to more modern ways. After World War II, the Japanese were buying everything in sight in America. In recent years, some of their investments have not turned out so good. Now, they have a problem with China. The Chinese economy is booming. I do not think Japan can keep up with them. China has the advantage because of their cheap labor. Today, the United States is the biggest buyer of Chinese goods. In ten years or less, China will be a very powerful country, even though they are still Communists.

How many zeros in a billion? When you hear a politician say "a billion" in a casual manner, think about whether you want him or her spend your tax money. One senator asked Congress for $250 billion dollars to rebuild New Orleans after Hurricane Katrina. If you are one of the 480,000 residents of New Orleans, you—along with every man, woman, and child—would receive $500,000. If you have one of the 180,000 homes in New Orleans, you get $1,300,000. If you are a family of four, you get $1,500,000. Here is how the government figures how to pay for it with your taxes:

- Accounts Receivables Tax
- Building Permit Tax
- Cell Phone Tax
- Cigarette Tax
- Corporate Income Tax
- Federal Income Tax
- Federal Unemployment Tax (FUTA)
- Dog License Tax
- Fishing License Tax
- Food License Tax
- Fuel Permit Tax
- Gasoline Tax
- Hunting License Tax
- Inheritance Tax
- Inventory Tax
- IRS Interest Charges (Tax on top of tax)

- Liquor Tax
- Luxury Tax
- Marriage License Tax
- Medicare Tax
- Property Tax
- Real Estate Tax
- Race Track Betting Tax
- Casino Winnings Tax
- Road Usage Tax
- Recreational Vehicle Sales Tax
- Social Security Tax
- Sales Tax
- State Income Tax
- State Unemployment Tax (SUTA)
- Telephone Federal Excise Tax
- Telephone Federal, State, and Local Surcharge Tax
- Telephone Minimum Usage Surcharge Tax
- Telephone Recurring and Nonrecurring Charges Tax
- Utility and Competition and Welfare Tax
- Vehicle License Registration Tax
- Vehicle Sales Tax
- Watercraft Registration Tax
- Well Permit Tax
- Workers Compensation

The politicians all want to get their hands on easy money. Back many years ago, none of these taxes existed. Our nation was debt-free, and we were the most prosperous country in the world. Now, the politicians are thinking about charging the public for the plastic bags we get at the stores. They sit up nights trying to think of ways to tax us more. We, the people, better start rejecting the politicians because socialism is in our backyard. This was a great country until all these socialistic immigrants slid their way into politics. Some of them want to take away our freedoms. They are making inroads in our society. I feel sorry for our younger generation; they do not realize they are losing their freedom, little by little, each day. I do not understand why our do-nothing politicians allow this to happen. The people have to take it and keep quiet. Wake up, America, and let's exercise our power and stop being politically correct to appease these Communists that are in our government and in the news media.

I am a senior, and I have seen many corrupt things go on in our government. I used to be proud of my government, but not anymore. I fought in World War II and was proud to fight and win for our country's freedom; it made me proud. Today, people talk against this country. If they do not like it here, why not go back where they came from? All I know is that millions of people keep coming here, legally or illegally. Getting back to our politicians, they do not care about the taxpayers. The politicians do not want term limits. Why should they vote themselves out of office? The only way we can do it is to demand that our congressmen or senators vote for this change. That will make them honest when they are in office. The only way we can get a handle on this situation is to have term limits. They have a tax code that is twelve thousand pages long. This is to keep the public confused. The politicians want it this way so that they can steal more money for their pet projects. That is how they get their cash kickbacks. There is only one way to solve this problem: have a flat tax. Everyone making over $50,000 should pay 15 percent of their income. Everyone making under $50,000 should be exempt from income taxes.

Now, we have President Obama in the White House. Let us see what he can do to stop these political gangsters from stealing the public's money. There is plenty of money to be had with this stimulus program. He said he will create three million more jobs. So far we have lost over a million jobs. Who is getting billions? Aig Insurance Co., that's who. And who do they hire? Citibank's also getting the money. How many employees do they hire? None. GM? They laid off thousands. I think President Obama is in lala land. In the meantime, the American taxpayer is going to pay for Obama's mistakes.

If there are any honest politicians left, they should scrutinize every program that involves money given out. If nothing is done to stop this giveaway program, this country is headed for disaster. People will be taxed on everything: food, cigarettes, cars, in addition to higher prices on electricity and other commodities. The so-called poor do not care. They will get extra checks. The working class will have to pay taxes for the rest of their lives.

Another bailout for GM—it is so simple to settle. If I was the CEO of GM, I would sit down with the head of the UAW and say, "Your workers have been making seventy-five dollars per hour plus benefits. That adds up to more than three thousand dollars per week. The Japanese produce better cars at half the cost. That's why GM is in trouble." I would tell the union leaders to either cut the employees by fifty percent or we would close down. The CEO can live without a job; can the workers? Sending more bailout money is not going to save GM. It is only going to make the public pay more.

Where has Al Gore been hiding lately? He will not show his face until July or August, when the temperature is in the nineties. Why not tell the people in the Midwest and East Coast about global warming. They just went through a very cold, snowy winter. I had a conversation with a scientist who claims that we are heading for a cooling period. The reason they do not speak out is that it is not politically correct now. Our EPA says that cows pass gas and that is bad for the environment. If that is the case, I am going into the cork business. That should be very profitable. If I were younger, I would consider it. Everyone on this planet should have a cork up their butt to prevent gas that damages our climate.

To get rid of corruption in DC, we should have term limits for congressmen and senators of four years.

CHAPTER 7

CONCLUSION

The goal I sought to achieve in writing this book was to make you laugh, cry, and experience what life was like back in the good old days. Maybe you can learn from my mistakes and successes so your journey through life will be as colorful as mine. As they say, history repeats itself. So take a good look at what has happened in the past, as it is a good predictor for what is to come.